Routledge Revivals

The Child in Context

First published in 1985, *The Child in Context* is the first to bring together the practice of educational psychology and the 'family-systems' theories regularly practised by psychologists, psychiatrists, and social workers in their attempt to understand the relationship between individuals and the social systems of which they are a part. The author, an educational psychologist herself, demonstrates how the educational psychologist can, in her efforts to help children who are failing in mainstream education, incorporate an understanding of family processes into her work with the child and his family. This integrative approach is also applied to the other system—the school—to which the child belongs, and to the interrelationship between different professionals involved in the management of the child.

This book was written in the wake of the 1981 Education Act, at a time when educational psychologists were increasing their contact with parents. The discussion is illustrated with examples from the writer's own experience with children of various ages and nationalities and covers a wide variety of behavioural and developmental difficulties.

The Child in Context

Family-Systems Theory in Educational Psychology

Jean Campion

ROUTLEDGE REVIVALS
Routledge
Taylor & Francis Group

First published in 1985
by Methuen & Co. Ltd

This edition first published in 2025 by Routledge
4 Park Square, Milton Park, Abingdon, Oxon, OX14 4RN

and by Routledge
605 Third Avenue, New York, NY 10017

Routledge is an imprint of the Taylor & Francis Group, an informa business

A Library of Congress record exists under LCCN:

ISBN: 978-1-041-04741-4 (hbk)
ISBN: 978-1-003-62973-3 (ebk)
ISBN: 978-1-041-04756-8 (pbk)

Book DOI 10.4324/9781003629733

The Child in Context

Family-systems theory in educational psychology

Jean Campion

METHUEN
London and New York

First published in 1985 by
Methuen & Co. Ltd
11 New Fetter Lane, London EC4P 4EE

Published in the USA by
Methuen & Co.
in association with Methuen Inc.
733 Third Avenue, New York, NY 10017

Filmset by Northumberland Press Ltd,
Gateshead, Tyne and Wear
Printed in Great Britain by
Richard Clay (The Chaucer Press) Ltd,
Bungay, Suffolk

British Library Cataloguing in Publication Data

Campion, Jean
The child in context: family-systems theory in educational psychology.
1. Problem children – Education
2. Parent and child
I. Title
371.94 LC4801

ISBN 0–416–39090–0
ISBN 0–416–39100–1 Pbk

Library of Congress Cataloging in Publication Data

Campion, Jean
The child in context

Bibliography: p.
Includes index.
1. Family psychotherapy. 2. Home and school.
3. Parent–student counselor relationships.
4. Problem children – Education. I. Title.
RC488.5C35 1985 371.4′6 84–27249
ISBN 0–416–39090–0
ISBN 0–416–39100–1 (pbk.)

Contents

1

Introduction

The 1981 Education Act is designed to provide extra help and support for children with special educational needs. These are children who, for one reason or another, are unable to benefit from, or adapt themselves to, the curriculum and facilities which are normally on offer in mainstream education. Such children have long been the concern of educational pyschologists, who must welcome the new Act and the attention it gives to many vulnerable children.

Understandably, though in many ways unfortunately, most of the publicity surrounding the Act has focused on those children who have a recognized and recognizable handicap that is physical in nature (e.g. deafness, spina bifida, mental handicap). It is therefore easy to overlook the fact that there is a much larger group of children who give cause for concern in mainstream education. These are children who, though not mentally retarded or physically handicapped, fail to make normal developmental progress with others of their age group. These children, who are well known to educational psychologists working the school psychological services, tend to be described in different ways by different professionals. In general terms, they are quite often behaviourally disturbed and socially immature; many have quite serious learning difficulties; some are depressed, and drift away from school. In secondary schools, such children are often (though not invariably) to be found in withdrawal groups or units, or in remedial classes. But it would be wrong to suppose that their difficulties can be attributed to the onset of adolescence, the experience of failure in the classroom, or the inadequacies of the education system. Most of these vulnerable children have difficulties which can be traced back to the infant or pre-school years. Equally, many infant and pre-school children are regularly referred with the same mixture of problems: social, emotional and cognitive. It is with these children and their families that this book is primarily concerned.

Parental involvement

One of the recommendations of the Education Act is that parents should be closely involved with the professionals if their child is felt to have a special educational need. This recommendation is to be welcomed, although it is already common practice for psychologists (and others) to co-operate whenever possible with the parents of a child who is referred for psychological assessment. In spite of this, it is unrealistic to pretend that the task of involving parents is without its difficulties, real or potential. In the first place, it is by no means always easy for parents to see the need to co-operate, particularly if they do not see anything 'wrong' with the child. This is particularly likely to be the case when the child's behaviour or performance is in question, rather than his physical condition. It must be remembered that parents themselves rarely seek the advice of a psychologist: almost invariably it is others (teachers, social workers, doctors, health visitors) who are concerned by the child's lack of progress or aberrant behaviour, and have persuaded the parents to allow a referral to be made. The psychologist, meeting the parents, recognizes the need to form a relationship with them, yet is aware that they probably have mixed feelings about her involvement, and little understanding of the nature of her role.

Nor is this the only difficulty for the psychologist who recognizes the importance and the value of working closely with the parents of a referred child. During family interviews, she may become aware that the child's problems, as observed in the classroom, are only one part of his difficulties. Parents may describe various problems at home which must have placed the child under strain for a number of years, and which must be taken into consideration as part of the process of diagnosis, remediation and treatment. Occasionally and unfortunately, parental attitudes towards the child seem unsatisfactory or inadequate for his developmental needs. The psychologist feels uneasy, yet recognizes that it is not her task to pass judgement on the parents or to criticize the way in which they lead their lives; rather, it is to co-operate with them to promote change in their child.

These are difficult and sometimes controversial topics, but they cannot be ignored. It is important that we should think of parents as partners in the task of helping the child to overcome his behavioural difficulties or to improve his performance in the classroom. At the same time, it is essential to take into consideration the possibility that certain family factors, or factors in the parent–child relationship, may be acting against the child's best interest, or putting a brake on his natural, healthy developmental progress. Nor can we pretend that collaborating with a child's parents in an attempt to help him is the same as collaborating with another adult. The relationship between parents and their children is unique: it has certain strengths and weaknesses which are quite different from any other adult–child relationship. It is the psychologist's task to be aware of these strengths and weaknesses, and to take them into consideration when deciding the best way to help a particular child.

It is suggested that the relationship that exists between the psychologist and parents of a referred child can usefully be considered – initially at least – under three separate headings: consultation, partnership and family therapy. These are described briefly and separately below, and are the subject of a more extensive examination and discussion in later chapters.

Consultation

This is the traditional model of parent–psychologist relationship. The child is believed to have a 'problem' which needs assessment and diagnosis, and the psychologist is consulted as an expert. Sometimes this consultation will be part of a total diagnostic process involving other professionals; at other times, the psychologist is the only professional involved.

In this model, the psychologist is the expert with certain skills and expertise which will be employed for the child's benefit. She also (usually) has access to certain facilities (educational or otherwise) which might be useful to the child. The parents, for their part, are expected to be willing and able to contribute certain information about the child which will allow the psychologist to make an effective diagnosis of the child's difficulties.

Consultation is often only the beginning of a series of events designed to help the child. It sometimes leads to a closer relationship between the psychologist and the parents, which may develop in different ways over a period of time. It also has validity as a relationship in its own right, made briefly for the purpose of exchange of information.

Partnership

This is a more recent model for the parent–psychologist relationship. The psychologist is deemed to have certain knowledge or expertise which can be imparted directly to the parents, who are then instructed in certain techniques which they can apply directly to their own child. In this model, the psychologist is not only diagnostician and consultant, but a teacher (of the parents) and a partner. The parents are considered to be both able and willing to learn certain skills imparted by the psychologist, and to apply them effectively for the child's benefit.

Family therapy

This technique is used by social workers, psychologists and psychiatrists in an attempt to help a behaviourally disturbed individual–child or adult. Certain behaviour patterns between family members are held to create or maintain (or both) disturbed or symptomatic behaviour in one or other members of a family – though family members are almost invariably unaware of the ways in which this is happening. This information cannot usually be imparted directly to the family, and the therapist is therefore involved in prompting 'systems change' indirectly, by whatever means seems most appropriate in the particular case.

In each of these three models, the psychologist–parent relationship takes a form that is fairly clearly distinguishable, and can be summarized as:

(1) consultant and client
(2) partners, with the parents learning directly from the psychologist
(3) therapist and clients.

Several questions must now be asked about the nature of these relationships, and about the ways in which they may be most effectively developed for the benefit of children.

First, is it possible for the *psychologist* to take on more than one role at a time? It might be suggested that, though all parent–psychologist relationships contain an element of consultation, partnership and therapy, they are totally different in nature, based on completely different models and involving separate and distinct skills on the part of the pyschologist. In some ways this is true, since psychologists can at times make a clear distinction between themselves as partners with the parents, or as therapists in family therapy. Indeed, many psychologists have been concerned to develop their skills in one or other of these areas (e.g. as therapists, *or* as instructors of parents in certain skills or techniques). On the other hand, the two approaches can sometimes be usefully combined for the benefit of the child, with the psychologist using her skills and understanding flexibly to meet the needs of individuals and of the family as a whole in whatever way seems most appropriate.

Second, is it possible, or useful, to think of *parents* as falling into categories: those who can be involved as partners in helping their children, and those who need 'treatment' in family therapy? Probably not, though parents obviously do vary greatly in their ability to meet their children's needs and promote their social, emotional and cognitive growth. Some – relatively few – are quite disastrously damaging to their children, usually for complex reasons associated with unsatisfactory experiences in their own early lives. Most parents, however, want to help their children and to do the best for them, and most can be helped by the psychologist to meet their children's needs more adequately, and to offer their children specific help where this is needed. Nevertheless, the psychologist does need to be aware of the complexity of the issues if parents are to be involved in schemes of whatever nature to help their children. It must be recognized that the relationship between some parents and their children is both anxious and fragile, even when both adults and children are doing their best to fulfil their obligations to each other.

Third, is it useful to divide the presenting *problems* into categories: those which need a family therapy approach, those which can be alleviated by involving the parents in a partnership scheme, and those which require some other method of treatment or remediation? In one sense, different problems in children seem to require different approaches. On the other hand, it is not uncommon to find that apparently dissimilar problems respond to similar treatments. And *all* referred children, regardless of the apparent nature of their difficulties, have similar developmental needs.

The theme of the book

The focus of this book is on families where one child has been referred to the educational psychologist as the result of behavioural disturbance, learning difficulties and/or lack of progress at school. I hope to be able to show that it is often possible to make links between the child's behaviour and performance at school and his experience within his family, and to use that knowledge flexibly and caringly for the benefit of both child and family. Although described as a family-systems method of helping children, it is both broader and more flexible than family therapy, and has a wider application. It is a method of helping children which can be used in addition to other, more traditional, methods used by psychologists to help behaviourally disturbed children, or children with learning difficulties in the classroom (e.g. behaviour modification, structured learning programmes). Its great strength is that it is able to take into consideration many different factors: in the child himself, in the family, and in the school.

The children whose cases are described in the book are known individually to the writer, though certain factual details in their case-histories have, for obvious reasons, been slightly altered or simplified. I have chosen not to discuss the physically or mentally handicapped child, since a discussion of such children needs to include a discussion of their particular handicap, which is beyond the scope of this book. There are, in any case, many excellent books written for psychologists who wish to involve the parents of such children in schemes to help them develop their strength and skills. Nevertheless, I would suggest that some of what is written about children and their families in this book is relevant to these children as well.

Indeed, it is suggested that much of what is written is relevant to all families. No family is without its problems, and few children are entirely problem-free throughout childhood and adolescence. In all families, individual members are continually affecting and being affected by other members of the family – for better or worse. Each family has its moments of stress, some of which pass quickly, while others leave their mark on some or all family members. Children grow and change, and parents must be able to grow and change too, and adapt themselves to the continually changing needs of their offspring.

Understanding the relevance of these, and other, factors allows the psychologist to work effectively with families for the benefit of children of all ages, regardless of the apparent nature of their problems.

Note

The cases described in the book are those of children known to the writer, although some of the details have been altered to preserve the anonymity of the children and their families.

In writing the book, I needed a different pronoun for the psychologist and the referred child for the sake of clarity and economy of expression. I hope that no particular significance will be attached to my choice of 'she' for the psychologist and 'he' for the referred child. Where actual cases are described, I have of course kept to the gender of the child concerned.

2

The children

Many children, for differing reasons, show signs of behavioural disturbance, developmental difficulties and/or learning problems from a young age. Some of these children will develop reasonably well, given perhaps some additional help and support, for example, help in the remedial department at school or the regular support of a school counsellor. Others will need much specialized, individual help and attention, perhaps for many years. The 1981 Education Act was designed to meet the needs of these children, though it is at present a little uncertain just how many of them actually fall within its provisions (i.e. *all* children with a behaviour problem or a learning difficulty, or only those with more serious developmental difficulties).

Children with learning difficulties and behaviour problems may be described in terms of their *educational* needs, but their problems frequently extend well beyond the classroom. They can be, and are, helped in different ways by different professionals: psychologists, social workers, teachers, psychiatrists, speech therapists, to name but a few. The goals of those involved are both specific and general. Thus the aim is to help the child overcome whatever specific difficulty of handicap he may have, whilst at the same time promoting and encouraging a more satisfactory, general, all-round development.

Some of the children will have a recognizable, physical disability or handicap – deafness, severe speech difficulties, partial sight, for example. Most, however, will not. The majority of children whose behaviour and/or performance give cause for concern to adults do not have a physical problem which could have contributed significantly to their difficulties. These difficulties are, nevertheless, very real, and the children need help if they are to overcome them at least partially, and make satisfactory developmental progress alongside their peers. It is suggested that these children can be described in broad terms under two separate headings: behaviour problems and learning difficulties. The categories are not, however, mutually exclusive. Many (probably most) children referred to the school psychological service are giving cause for concern to their teachers and others because both their behaviour *and* their performance in the classroom (and often elsewhere) appears unsatisfactory or inadequate.

Behavioural disturbance in children

The term 'behavioural disturbance' is popularly associated with the difficult, obstreperous, aggressive behaviour of certain adolescents. But the term is also used to describe a wide variety of behaviours in children which might be described as 'significantly different' from the behaviour of other children of the same age group. These include withdrawn, confused behaviour, anxious, neurotic behaviour, socially immature behaviour, as well as the more inconvenient 'acting-out'. It is equally applicable to the infant school child who responds inappropriately to the teacher's requests and suggestions, and fails to make relationships with other children, as it is to the aggressive secondary school child.

It has been suggested that behavioural disturbance in children arises from a continual experience of failure at school. While this might be true in some cases, this suggestion ignores the fact that there are a large number of pre-school children who also show signs of behavioural disturbance. Richman *et al.* (1982) found that a quarter of a large sample (705) of 3-year-olds had behaviour problems, and that 75 per cent of these children had not outgrown their problems by the age of 8. McMichael (1979) demonstrated that a large number of non-reading infant school children had entered school with poor social skills, and regarded as highly questionable the theory that anti-social behaviour arose from the experience of failure associated with a lack of ability to read.

Traditional models for describing and alleviating behavioural disturbance in children are derived from *psychoanalytic theory* based on the works of Sigmund Freud, and on the experiences and theories of those who developed and elaborated his original models of normal and abnormal human behaviour. Freud described the personality of the individual as divisible into three interacting parts: the id, ego and super-ego. The id contains or represents the immediate, bodily needs and impulses of the individual, the ego is the reality principle, and the super-ego the mechanism of self-control (or internalized moral code). The psychological task for the individual is that of gradually developing ego strengths and super-ego control, while subduing (or incorporating into the ego) the more primitive urges of the id. While this is taking place, the child passes through different stages of development: the oral, anal and phallic. Each stage – and the transition from stage to stage – brings with it for the child some degree of conflict and anxiety, as the processes of socialization (e.g. weaning, toilet–training, acquiring socially acceptable behaviour) take place. In Freud's view, neurotic (behavioural) disturbance in both children and adults can be traced back to anxiety associated with this early period of development, and varies according to the degree of conflict experienced, its nature, and the stage at which the conflict took place. (See Freud, 1923.)

Freud also described the mechanism of 'defence', by which the individual attempts to avoid the need to 'face up to' certain anxiety-provoking realities. Thus, certain thoughts may be *repressed* (to give rise to symptoms at a later date), *denied* ('forgotten'), *projected* (so that internal anxieties are seen as having an external cause) or dealt with by the process of *reaction-formation* (where the individual expresses the opposite to what he is 'really' feeling, to avoid anxiety associated with real feelings). These mechanisms are unconscious, although people can sometimes become aware of them if they are pointed out. It is easier to see the defences of others than one's own!

It is arguable that Freud's concept of defence is more useful in a practical sense to educational psychologists than his theories of the anxieties associated with the early years of life (although these, too, are useful in my view). It is not uncommon to see children take refuge in defensive attitudes (e.g. denying blame or shifting it on to others, denying suffering, or blows to their pride) although one needs to be able to distinguish between unconscious defences and deliberate lie-telling. It is quite often the case that the child's ability to be helped depends on his ability and willingness to recognize his own culpability, weaknesses and sufferings (see Freud, A., 1937).

Psychoanalytic theory has been so long associated with Freud that it is easy to forget the contributions of others. The work of Melanie Klein has probably been undervalued as a means of understanding and helping both individual children and adults, as well as groups and families. Klein presented a complex theory of the very early stages of the baby's development (i.e. the first year of life). She suggested that the baby passes through essential developmental phases during this period as he gradually becomes aware of his separateness (separate identity) from his mother. The very early, first stage of development, which Klein calls the *paranoid–schizoid position*, is a state of confusion in which the child is uncertain of the boundaries which exist between himself and his mother. This stage gives way to what Klein calls the *depressive position*: the baby becomes aware of his separate identity, and also gradually comes to terms with the knowledge that the mother who cares for him and loves him is the same person as the mother who occasionally frustrates, denies or rejects him. This coming to terms with reality and relinquishing, at least in some measure, an egocentric and omnipotent view of the world is an essential part of the process of personality development.

Klein's theories are rich and complex, and sometimes difficult to understand and accept. Perhaps most readily acceptable is her description of the way in which the process of 'splitting' takes place. That is to say, the individual who has found it difficult to reconcile the idea of both the 'good' and 'bad' mother may find it difficult to see both good and bad in other individuals, and situations, later in life, tending instead to see the world in extremes of black and white, rather than in shades of grey. It is, perhaps, a difficulty which many people experience to a greater or lesser extent. (Readers who are unfamiliar with Klein's works should read *Our Adult World* (1963) before embarking on her studies of children in psychoanalysis.)

Both Freud and Klein were primarily concerned with the *internal* processes and experiences of the child, rather than with external influences – although they were not unaware of the importance of these. However, others in the psychoanalytic movement have paid greater attention to *external* factors, in particular the attitudes of the child's parents (primarily the mother) towards the child. Anna Freud, for example, suggests that parental neglect, seduction of the child, inaccessibility to the child, and inappropriate responses all contribute to creating conflict and behavioural disturbance, in addition to whatever conflict the child may be experiencing associated with his developmental growth and change (see Freud, A., 1981), and Bowlby (1979) stresses the importance of a loving bond (attachment) between the mother and the child as a foundation for successful social and emotional development in the child. Winnicott (1965a and b) describes the development of the child in the context of certain harmful influences within the family (e.g. the adverse effects of living with parents whose personalities are disturbed or disordered), and stresses that the child needs to be able to experience his separate identity, while at the same time having his needs adequately catered for, and his anxieties understood and 'held' by a loving but not over-intrusive parent. Theories which focus on the very early years of life are hard either to prove or disprove. However, we are increasingly aware of the importance of this period, and of the social and emotional interactions which take place between mother and child (e.g. see Schaffer, 1977; Stern, 1977), and it is now clear that the learning which takes place at this time is crucial to the child's subsequent development.

Psychodynamic psychology and psychiatry are associated with individual psychotherapy and psychoanalysis as treatment methods for neurotic (behavioural) disturbance. In the case of children, treatment may be offered via the parents, who are helped to achieve some degree of insight into the child's problems, and some awareness of ways in which they might improve their own attitudes towards him. It is, however, important to remember that psychodynamic theories are regularly incorporated into clinical and other interpersonal work with both children and adults; that is, in family therapy and in counselling (Noonan, 1984). The value of understanding certain concepts (e.g. those of 'defence' and Klein's description of 'splitting') has already been mentioned. In other words, it is possible to draw on psychoanalytic theory widely and flexibly rather than assuming that they belong exclusively to the world of psychoanalysis and individual child psychotherapy.

Although many educational psychologists do draw on these theories, the discipline of educational psychology as a whole owes more to *behaviourism* than to psychoanalytic theory (though with an increasing interest in developmental psychology there may be a shift in emphasis). The behaviourist stance of many, even most, psychologists arises from (a) an academic training in behavioural and experimental psychology, (b) an impatience with the often complex and long-drawn-out treatment methods associated with child psychiatry, and (c) the need for pyschologists to establish themselves and their discipline as separate from psychiatry, and perhaps in some ways superior to it.

The behaviourist model will be familiar to the reader, and it is not necessary to do more than outline the theory and its applications. Behaviourist principles are based on learning theory as demonstrated and described by Pavlov, Hull, Thorndike, and others. Certain actions may take place as a 'conditioned response' to a particular stimulus; they also arise as a result of accident or trial-and-error, and will be repeated if 'reinforced' by a result which is pleasurable or anxiety-reducing to the individual. Thus, certain actions tend, over a period of time, to become part of the repertoire of the individual and are incorporated into his personality. Behavioural disturbance is seen in terms of learnt (maladaptive) behaviour patterns, which need to be unlearnt, and the psychologist (probably) shows little interest in knowing the reasons for the child's behaviour in terms of internal conflicts or anxieties.

Although behaviourism focuses principally on theories of reinforcement, attention is also paid to social factors. Children are known to copy certain actions and attitudes, and to change their behaviour to conform to the actions of adult and peer-group models (see Bandura, 1971; Sarason, 1978). Recently, too, behaviourists have applied learning-theory principles to the modification of cognitive processes (Meichenbaum, 1977). Thus, children are helped to overcome their problems by giving themselves verbal instructions, or verbal rewards on occasions, when a task (e.g. self-control in a particular situation) is successfully accomplished.

A behaviourist approach to helping children overcome behaviour problems emphasizes the need to observe in some detail the behaviour which one hopes to modify or change, and also to observe those factors or situations which precede or trigger the undesirable action(s). Equally, it is important to observe the consequences which flow from the actions. By focusing on the

'ABC' (antecedent/behaviour/consequence) of behavioural disturbance, the psychologist's aim is to plan an intervention which will change the sequence (see Herbert, 1981). For example, a child may always misbehave when his mother attends to the needs of his baby brother. His misbehaviour brings parental attention, even though that attention takes the form of a reprimand. The psychologist might suggest to the parent that she reward the child in a more positive way by playing with him when his brother is asleep, and commenting on his 'good' behaviour when it occurs; and avoid attending to the baby at particularly sensitive moments (e.g. when the older child arrives home from school).

Behaviourist principles are regularly applied in schools, of course, both formally and informally. Children receive rewards in the form of praise or a gold star from their teachers for tasks successfully completed, or for 'good' behaviour. Educational psychologists regularly help teachers to design behaviour modification programmes as part of their classroom management, particularly where there are difficult or disruptive pupils (see Presland, 1974, 1980). This does not mean that teachers and psychologists do not recognize the need to understand certain anxieties or conflicts in children as well. Thus a behavioural approach is often supplemented by techniques such as counselling, group or play therapy, all of which owe much to psychoanalytic theory. Indeed, it is probably true to say that there is no real conflict between the two apparently different approaches. A 'unit' of behaviour can be said to arise from conflict or anxiety within the individual; equally, it will tend to be repeated if its expression results in a pleasurable, or anxiety-reducing reinforcement (Dollard and Miller, 1950; Wachtel, 1977; Marmor and Woods, 1980). At times it is more helpful and appropriate to encourage or promote some degree of insight in the child as to the reasons for his disturbed or disruptive behaviour. At other times it is more appropriate to help him overcome it by a programme of behaviour modification.

Alternatively, it may be more helpful to focus attention on family or school systems of which the child is a part.

The most recent trend in educational psychology is that of *developmental psychology*. Still in its infancy as a separate discipline, developmental psychology draws on many different models and theories: behavioural, dynamic, biological, systemic. Each model makes a contribution to the whole picture of the developing child—a picture which is immensely rich and complex. Thus the child's behaviour (in the broadest sense of the word) is seen as the result of many different experiences dating back to the early years or months of life. His personality develops as a result of many different interactions, within the child and between the child and his environment, and as the result of adaptations which he makes to certain experiences in his life, including parental attitudes, relationships with siblings and peers, and environmental stress. It is also, in a different but in no way contradictory sense, the result of learning as described by the learning theorists. In the case of behaviourally disturbed children it is frequently and unfortunately the case that both the learning and the environmental influences have been either unsatisfactory or insufficient for his developmental needs.

Does the *child* have the problem?

Many people concerned to help behaviourally disturbed children have resisted the suggestion that the child has a 'problem' in the sense that the problem belongs to, or is part of, his own personality. They would claim that children who behave in a wild, violent or disruptive way do so because they are inappropriately treated by adults, not because they are disturbed or maladjusted. Educational psychologists have been to the fore in this approach, which has focused increasingly on understanding the ways in which schools can, by looking at the ways in which they handle and teach their children, promote co-operative and acceptable attitudes in the children themselves (see Gillham, 1978).

There are several important influences in the field of systems theory, some of which will be mentioned during the course of this book. Here, it is important to recognize the contribution of R. D. Laing (1970), who suggested that it is always impossible to understand the (disturbed) behaviour of an individual without referring to the patterns of behaviour which prevail in the individual's family. Laing's concern was with adult psychiatry, and his method of helping psychiatric patients included wherever possible attention to family attitudes and communications. It was frequently apparent that these attitudes tended to produce, or to maintain, symptomatic behaviour in the individual. This suggestion was a radical move away from the idea that the person with the symptoms was the one in whom the problem resided. The implications of this theory are considerable, and will be discussed more fully in a later chapter.

Social interaction (S.I.) theory is a rather different view of behavioural disturbance, which nevertheless stresses the importance of social (group) experiences on the behaviour of an individual. Tattum (1982) describes this theory in the following terms: 'Man does not simply react: he evaluates, criticises, defines, and then acts in the light of his own interpretation and construction of reality.' This viewpoint is important, but it does perhaps suggest a greater degree of detachment and self-control than is often found in human behaviour. Perhaps the most important factor is the recognition that, although the child may be said to have a problem in one sense, if his behaviour is continually unpredictable, confused, violent or withdrawn, it is *equally* true to say that the child's behaviour is constantly being modified and changed (for better or worse) by adult actions and attitudes. Some adults are good at handling 'difficult' children, and some are not. Thus, the child's problems will tend either to diminish or to increase with the passage of time.

There can, of course, never be any hard-and-fast rules about what is 'normal' and what is 'abnormal': children (like adults) can be truculent, disagreeable, tearful, without necessarily being abnormal – indeed, this kind of behaviour is often a *normal* reaction to an abnormal (e.g. stressful) situation. This is not, however, to deny that certain children give serious cause for concern to adults interested in their welfare. And rightly so.

In summary, it is suggested that the following concepts are useful in describing behaviourally disturbed children.

(1) A child's behaviour, learnt over a period of time, has meaning in terms of his life-experience and his experience of himself as an individual.
(2) The child's behaviour often represents considerable conflict and anxiety. Behaviourally disturbed children have often lived with rejection, confusion and emotional neglect so that their self-esteem and their self-control is poor.
(3) A child's apparently abnormal behaviour may sometimes be a normal response to a stressful situation. It is, for example, normal for children to show anger or despair following, say, a parental separation; normal for them to take up defensive attitudes against unhelpful adult attitudes; normal for them to test adult limits, and to be difficult or negative at times.
(4) Adult reaction to behaviourally disturbed children is a vital factor in either discouraging or (unwittingly) perpetuating the child's actions.
(5) Behaviourally disturbed children are probably best helped by some attention to their needs as an individual, *and* attention to the weaknesses of the family and school systems which include the child.

Learning difficulties

Most children who are referred to the school psychological services have in some measure difficulty in learning when compared with others of the same age group. Unfortunately, however, the term 'learning difficulties' can be applied to many children with different problems and different educational and social needs – to the slow learning child of below average intelligence, the child of average ability who, for social and emotional reasons, has fallen behind other children, and to the highly intelligent child who has a specific reading and writing problem.

We are at present concerned principally with children who fall (broadly) in the last two categories. That is to say, they are of average, or above average intelligence, yet fail to make the progress in reading and writing which one would normally expect of a child of that age and ability. It is probably true to say that even more controversy exists over the subject of learning difficulties than over the subject of behaviour problems. This is particularly the case with specific learning difficulties (i.e. in one area, such as reading) in otherwise intelligent children. Some would claim that a severe learning difficulty reflects psychological, and perhaps neurological, dysfunction of a highly specific nature, and that the child should be helped by a structured learning programme based on remediation of his apparent weakness. On the other hand, some pyschologists are more inclined to the view that, since the link between brain and behaviour is so imperfectly understood by both neurologists and psychologists, a more flexible approach to helping the child is indicated, and they would probably prefer to use techniques of remediation which are based on good infant and junior school teaching methods, with a programme geared as much to the child's interests and abilities as to his apparent weaknesses. In my view, this latter approach is more useful. It recognizes that the child's difficulty probably arises from a multitude of different factors and processes: social and emotional, as well as cognitive and (possibly) physical. It allows the teacher to build on his or her own expertise developed over a period of time as the result of helping children with similar problems – in short it is a creative as well as a scientific approach.

A flexible approach to the problem of learning difficulties also has the advantage of avoiding the considerable pitfalls associated with fixed labels. Much fruitless discussion can take place between adults on the subject of whether or not a particular child is dyslexic, for example. Regardless of the fundamental reason for a particular learning difficulty, if it is seen by adults to be comparable with, say, colour blindness or a physical illness, the psychologist's ability to help the child may well be diminished.

It is arguable that insufficient attention has been paid to understanding the relationship which exists between social and emotional development, and cognitive development, which includes the development of symbolic functioning. The relationship is probably close, and may well start at a very early stage in life. It is accepted, in a general sense, that children need a satisfactory social and emotional experience during the early years of life if they are to make successful all-round development, also that the child derives certain essential benefits from a good relationship with a parent-figure in the early months of life (see e.g. Stern, 1977). However, the detail of the developmental process and of the relationship between social experience and cognitive development are as yet imperfectly understood: Lidz (1978) suggested that the child's ability to develop successful symbolic functioning could be compared with his ability to achieve and maintain a discrete and integrated personality, and that both attributes were largely dependent on a satisfactory social and emotional experience within the family during the early years of life; Rubinstein and Levitt (1977) suggested that maternal psychopathology might make it impossible for a child to establish adequate communication with others – communication which is a necessary element in learning; and Coghill and colleagues found a relationship between maternal depression following childbirth and learning difficulties in the child at a later date. This is a complex and controversial field of discussion. However, the most important, emerging factor is that the child's *total* experience needs to be considered in any attempt to alleviate his learning problems.

It is arguable that too much attention has been given to the learning problem itself as it appears 'on paper', and too little to vital aspects of the child's experience – including his self-concept, relationships with others, his thoughts and anxieties. There is also a tendency to separate factors which are probably closely related (for example, to speak of the child as having an emotional/social problem *and* a learning difficulty, instead of describing one as a facet of the other). Relatively few educational psychologists and teachers have attempted to look at the relationship between learning problems/reading difficulties and emotional disturbance in children, as Chazan (1982) notes. Nor, indeed, have they given much attention to considering them in relation to the child's social and emotional development. (If they have, their findings have been poorly documented.) Notable exceptions to this include Ravenette (1979), who stresses the importance of looking beyond the child's performance in reading, towards a consideration of his relationship with, and perception of, others and his self-concept; and Caspari (1974) whose writings form the basis of educational therapy (a remedial technique in reading which recognizes the need to understand the child's emotional resistance to reading, and in helping him overcome it).

It seems very likely that an increasing interest in the pre-school years, and the topic of developmental psychology, will focus attention on learning problems as part of the total developmental process in the child. For example, in their longitudinal study of children aged 3 to 8 years, Richman *et al.* (1982) found that pre-school children who had experienced domestic upset in the early years of their lives and were emotionally disturbed, tended to show language delay and, later, reading difficulties.

In summary, it is suggested that learning difficulties in children, like behavioural difficulties, may well arise from a number of factors, within the child and within the environment. It is therefore suggested that the psychologist can always usefully consider the child's *total* experience (including his personality and his relationship with others) when assessing and attempting to alleviate his learning difficulties, in addition to studying the child's observable and measurable performance.

Helping children: the psychologist's role

Children are referred to the school psychological services with a wide variety of problems associated with disturbed (or disturbing) behaviour, unsatisfactory general development and/or learning difficulties. It is the task of the individual psychologist to try to meet the needs of such children to the best of her ability by whatever means seems most appropriate. There are, however, rarely any obvious solutions to a child's problems, and many different factors need to be taken into consideration by the psychologist who is trying to help an individual child. These include:

(1) the nature of the child's problem as it appears to
 - (a) the psychologist following observation of the child and individual psychological assessment
 - (b) the referring agent (e.g. the school)
 - (c) the child's parents

(2) family factors, including
 - (a) parental attitudes
 - (b) the apparent willingness of parents to be involved with the psychologist over a period of time
 - (c) family stress factors which might be adversely affecting the child

(3) educational factors, including
 - (a) the nature of the school attended by the child (e.g. its structure, its ethos, its resources)
 - (b) additional educational resources available to the child

(e.g. extra help outside the school, special groups and units, special education)

(4) other factors, including
   (a) the availability or non-availability of other resources (e.g. social workers, psychotherapy, etc.)
   (b) personal factors related to the psychologist's own interests, workload, etc.

Thus, to take a practical example, a psychologist who is faced with the problem of helping a child with a severe behaviour problem in the classroom may need to choose between (a) behaviour modification in the classroom, (b) group therapy for the child, (c) individual psychotherapy, (d) family therapy, and (e) recommending a special group or unit outside the school. In making this choice, the psychologist will inevitably be influenced by (i) the nature of the child's problem, (ii) the attitudes of staff at the school and the nature of the school system, (iii) the willingness, or otherwise, of parents to be involved in the psychologist's efforts to help the child (e.g. to attend family therapy sessions), and (iv) the existence or non-existence of extra facilities (groups, units, etc.).

This perhaps illustrates in some measure the complexity and the reality of the situation. It is rarely a question of applying any one treatment to a child with a specific problem. Although this approach can sometimes create a rather confusing situation, it also has its advantages. There are many *different* ways of helping children, and the psychologist almost invariably has a range of options available to her. The effectiveness of the help offered to the child depends on many factors, one of which is the relationship which the psychologist manages to establish with the child's parents.

3

Consultation

The traditional meeting-point for parents and psychologist is based on a recognition of the psychologist as an expert who must be consulted for an assessment of the child, and a diagnosis of his apparent difficulties. The expectation is that the psychologist will, during the course of consultation, make certain observations about the child, perhaps give certain facts and figures, and make a recommendation which will help the child overcome his difficulties.

The consultation model in its pure form is based on certain assumptions, most of which are borrowed from traditional medical models of human behaviour and development. The underlying assumption is that the child has, or may have, a condition which needs a particular form of treatment or remediation and that this condition and the treatment can be explained more or less directly to the child's parents. Yet this approach to helping children with behavioural difficulties and learning problems has been shown to be largely unhelpful in educational psychology (see Gillham, 1978). Few children who reach the educational psychologist for help have a specific and recognizable condition requiring a recognized form of treatment or remediation. They are, nevertheless, often in need of considerable help if they are to make reasonably satisfactory progress alongside their peers.

The consultancy model in its pure form is further complicated by the fact that, unlike a consultation with a doctor, it is rarely the parents themselves who have asked to see a psychologist. Most children are referred because someone other than the parents have seen that his behaviour and performance differ significantly from that of other children in the same age group. Occasionally, parents have to be persuaded over a period of time that the child needs help. Even when they are enthusiastic about the idea of a referral to the pyschologist, they may not necessarily agree with others about the *reasons* why their child should be referred. The fact is that the parents' view of the purpose of the assessment and the nature of the child's problem may be quite different from the viewpoint of others concerned with the child (teachers, health visitors).

As a starting-point for this discussion, two examples are given of children referred to an educational psychologist working in a school psychological service.

Kevin, aged 10, is falling badly behind his peers. He is described as confused and anxious. The headmaster has told his parents that he feels Kevin is under-achieving, and that a psychological assessment will help the teachers understand his difficulties. However, he has not commented on Kevin's behavioural disturbance, since he knows that the father himself is very anxious about Kevin, and rather punitive in his approach to the boy. Kevin's father is angry with the school – an anger based partly on Kevin's failure, and partly on his general dislike of schools dating back to his own educational failure as a child. Kevin's mother has recently seen a programme on dyslexia on the television, and has confused ideas about the possibility that he may be 'gifted'.

Even before the consultation takes place, it is apparent that the starting-point for each adult – and their expectations – is quite different: the father is ready to blame the school; the mother wants to look for a 'cure'; the headmaster is uneasy about the father's relationship with Kevin, and about his negative attitude to staff at the school. The psychologist, meeting the parents, is also anxious about this, but hopes to make a reasonable relationship with the parents, nevertheless. Later, she becomes aware that Kevin is not particularly intelligent, although the mother feels sure that he is.

Sara, aged 8, is referred by the school for aggressive behaviour in the classroom. The psychologist discovers she is in the care of the local authority and is fostered. There is a telephone call from social services to say that they feel the fostering arrangement is not going too well, and that they are not happy about the foster-parents. The foster-parents want to keep Sara but are afraid that she will be placed in special education. When the pyschologist meets the foster-parents, she too has some doubts about their ability to care for Sara, yet feels it might be possible to improve the relationship between them and the child. The teachers are at their wits' end and feel they cannot keep Sara at the school any longer, and put pressure on the psychologist to recommend an alternative educational placement.

In this case too the starting-points and the expectations of the adults concerned with helping Sara are different. The pyschologist needs to keep in mind the foster-parents' attitude, while at the same time being aware that Sara is in care, and may not stay with that family for much longer. She also needs to keep the teachers' viewpoint in mind, while not being hurried into making recommendations which would further upset a child who has obviously experienced many disruptions in her life. The psychologist's relationship with the social worker who has overall responsibility for Sara's welfare is equally important. Should she, for example, attempt to work with Sara's foster-parents in connection with Sara's educational difficulties, or should this be left to the social worker?

These examples are fairly typical of the type of case that regularly reaches the educational psychologist working in the school psychological service. The straightforward consultancy model cannot easily be applied on its own since all the adults concerned with the children have their own different anxieties, assumptions and expectations of the psychologist. These factors have an important part to play in the diagnosis of the child's apparent difficulty and the recommendations that the psychologist will eventually make to help the child.

It is useful to look at the different factors associated with consultancy under separate headings:

(1) the referral route
(2) the parents' understanding of the reason for psychological assessment and the psychologist's role
(3) the parents' understanding of the nature of the child's problem
(4) the psychologist's understanding of the child's problem.

The referring agency

Most children are referred to the school psychological services by schools with parental permission; some are referred by social services, or by the child psychiatric departments and clinics; others are referred by medical officers, speech therapists or, occasionally, by the parents themselves. Although the goal in all cases is that of achieving a greater understanding of the nature of the child's difficulties and, whenever possible, extra help for the child, each referring agency will have its own expectations of the educational pyschologist.

It cannot, unfortunately, be claimed that all referrals are always in the best interests of the child, much as one would like this to be the case. Some children are referred because a school is insufficiently flexible in its structure to meet the needs of children who are somewhat 'different', and a referral is made in the hope that the child will be placed in another school. Some are referred because other professionals are uncertain about the next step they should take in a particularly difficult case, and the help of the psychologist is requested almost *faute de mieux*. Some are referred because the expectations of adults (sometimes, unfortunately, the parents) are unreaslistically high. This is, of course, a pessimistic view. It is given because it cannot *automatically* be assumed that a referral to the educational psychologist is necessarily best for a particular child in that it adds anything useful to the diagnostic picture, or changes anything in his life. However, the educational psychologist is usually aware of this, and tries to make sure, by building up a relationship with the referring agencies (usually schools), that others have a realistic understanding of the nature of psychological assessment – including its limitations.

It is quite often the case that several different professionals (teacher, social worker, doctor, psychologist) are involved over a period of time with the same child. Although this can be helpful (indeed, it is often essential) it can also create some degree of confusion and misunderstanding. Sometimes this arises as the result of the different professional (working) models, and the terminology associated with those models which are used by the professionals. At other times, it arises because people have different anxieties about, and responsibilities to the child in question. Thus the psychologist may be worried by the child's general immaturity, a social worker by the home situation, the class teacher by the child's tendency to aggressive behaviour towards other children, and the parents by the child's slow academic progress.

These problems are not, of course, insurmountable, but they can make for certain problems in the parent–psychologist relationship. What, for example, have others said to the child's parents when they recommended a referral to the educational psychologist? Unfortunately, it is not uncommon to find that parents have been misled about the reasons for referral (usually inadvertently, of course). A parent might, perhaps, think that he or she is meeting the psychologist to discuss a child's reading difficulties, when the child's teachers are actually much more concerned about his behaviour problems.

Psychologists do, of course, need to speak to all the professionals who are concerned with a particular child, as well as to the child's parents. There is not usually any difficulty about this, although particular care may have to be taken if the parents have referred their child directly to the psychologist. But most parents readily give permission for contact with others to be made.

Parents' understanding of the psychologist's role

The way in which the parents understand the psychologist's role depends partly on the information they have been given by others (e.g. teachers, doctors) and partly on their concept of psychology. Some may confuse it with psychiatry. Others will have read about – or seen television programmes about – IQ testing, reading problems or mental handicap, where educational psychology has been mentioned. A parent may have had past experiences himself, good or bad, with the school psychological service or a child guidance clinic, or even have been in special education himself as a child.

Most parents expect tests of some kind to be applied to their child, and are happy for the psychologist to spend some time alone with the child. It is relatively common, following an individual assessment, for the parents to ask what is 'wrong' with the child – an understandable question, perhaps, but one which can rarely be answered in a sentence. Parents will often have their own ideas about the nature of the child's difficulties, ideas which can take the psychologist by surprise. For example, a parent might have genuine fears that their slightly immature child is seriously retarded and needs special education when such a thought has not crossed the psychologist's mind.

The parents' own deep-seated and long-standing anxieties about themselves, their families and their children can affect their attitude to the psychologist. They might not feel able to ask the psychologist the questions which are worrying them. On the other hand, they might not understand the reason for certain questions which the psychologist feels compelled to ask *them*. At times, the parents may appear defensive, angry or upset for reasons which are not always clear. These and other factors need to be handled sensitively by the psychologist when she first meets the parents if she is to gain their confidence and encourage them to continue to co-operate with her.

Occasionally, the parent sees the psychologist in an authoritarian role – for example, as one who will apply pressure to a truanting child, or dictate certain teaching methods to teachers. It may take a little time for parents to realize that this is not the psychologist's role.

The parents' view of the child's problem

Parents are inevitably very involved with their children, and often find it hard to take an objective view of their child's behaviour and performance, either at home or at school. Even if they do see the child more or less as others see him, they may not be willing to admit to others that they are anxious about his behaviour or his general development. At times, parents may become angry when faced with the reality of the child's problem, or perhaps take refuge in blaming others for his failure, his poor performance, or his behavioural difficulties.

Parents' own educational experience in many cases affects their attitude to their children's problems. Those parents who had special education themselves may be particularly anxious to avoid it for their children – either because they remember the comparatively ill-equipped special schools of the past, or because they are upset that their own 'problem' is also present in the child. On the other hand, parents who had no difficulty at all at school themselves may be quite unable to understand why their child cannot read, conform or make progress.

Sometimes there appear to be marked discrepancies between the parents' perception of the child and the view of the teacher or the psychologist. It is not unusual to be told by a parent that the child can read, for example, when others see no evidence of this. And the parents of quite severely handicapped children will sometimes, understandably perhaps, be unable to see the gap between their own child's performance and that of others of the same age group until, perhaps, a younger sibling begins to overtake the handicapped child.

Parents of children described as behaviourally disturbed in the classroom often claim that the child is no trouble at home – and this is often, of course, the case. Children do not necessarily behave in the same way in different environments. Indeed, the fact that the child appears to behave differently in certain settings is important information for the psychologist.

Occasionally, the parents' view of what is normal child behaviour is a little unusual. Certain parents appear genuinely puzzled when teachers are worried by the passive, silent behaviour of their child – behaviour which they see as both normal and desirable.

The psychologist's understanding of the nature of the child's problem

Although the psychological assessment of children follows, in theory, certain well-recognized patterns, each psychologist has a slightly different approach to the problem. Few would regard it as simply a question of measuring the child's performance on certain standardized tests. Most have developed techniques for understanding children which they use to supplement formal testing – techniques based on detailed observation of the child's behaviour, projective testing, conversation and play with the child, and discussion of the child's behaviour with adults in close contact with him. It is a question of gathering as much information as possible about the child before planning strategies which are designed to help him.

Psychologists do, however, vary in the importance they place on the information received about, and from, a particular child.

They may also vary in the way in which they interpret this information. Some psychologists rely more heavily on standardized tests than others; some are particularly sensitive to a child's social and emotional development, others perhaps less so. Differences between psychologists do not necessarily matter very much in the long run since there are several ways of approaching the task of understanding and helping children. However, apparent differences between psychologists can be a source of misunderstanding and confusion. For example, parents may receive apparently conflicting information on the topic of learning difficulties from two different psychologists, although the end result, in terms of help offered to the child, may well be similar.

In the past, an educational psychologist's description of a child was somewhat circumscribed by the need to place that child in a certain special education category if he was to receive extra help (e.g. maladjusted, ESN). These categories have been discarded in favour of a 'Statement of Needs' under the new Education Act. Although it is too early to say how the Act will affect children who seem to need more than is normally offered in mainstream education, it seems likely that psychologists will continue to be influenced by the nature of the range of options available to help a child, as well as by the nature of the child's difficulties. Decisions have to be taken about children at a practical level, and with the child's best *total* interests in mind: social, emotional and cognitive.

The relevance of consultation between parent and psychologist

For various reasons it would appear that consultation between a child's parents and the educational psychologist can never (or rarely) have the same quality as, say, consultation between parents and doctor on the subject of a child's hearing loss. There are too many conflicting viewpoints about the child, too many variables, and too much uncertainty to make this possible. Although the psychologist often does have certain *factual* information to impart to the parents – for example, on the subject of the child's performance compared with others, and the range of options available to help him – this information is often less important than other more complex factors associated with the child's failure, or his developmental difficulties. Nevertheless, consultation between parents and psychologist does have an important role to play as part of the process of helping the child. Indeed, once the limitations of the relationship are recognized, its full value can be exploited in a rather different direction.

Perhaps the most important aspect of consultation is that it gives the parents the opportunity to talk to someone whose task it is to understand children, and child development; to ask questions and to express anxieties in the knowledge that they will be treated seriously and with respect. Equally, and related to this, it gives the psychologist the opportunity to ask certain questions of the parents: questions designed to help her understand the child a little better.

Consultation can lay the foundation for a relationship between parent and psychologist which is both practical and therapeutic. If parental co-operation can be obtained at this early stage, a relationship can develop over a period of time in one of a number of directions, with lasting benefit to the child. The way in which this can come about will be described during the course of the book.

4

Parents as partners

The 1981 Education Act stresses the need for professionals who are involved in the assessment of children with a special educational need to regard the parents as partners in the process of assessment and decision-making. However, the term 'partnership with parents' has a rather different and more specific meaning in educational psychology. It has for some time been used to describe a relatively long-term relationship between a psychologist and the parents of a child whose behaviour or performance gives cause for concern, during which the parents learn certain techniques from the psychologist to apply to their own child.

Probably the most well-known and well-documented of these schemes are those in which psychologists have encouraged parents of quite severely physically or mentally handicapped children to help their own children (see e.g. Cameron, 1982). The work is based on the principles of learning theory. The child's behaviour and performance (which may well be at a very simple and immature level) is analysed in some detail as a starting-point for helping the child. Parents are taught to focus on one aspect of the child's behaviour or performance (for example, feeding himself) and to aim at improving it by a system of rewards. The task is broken down into its component parts: holding the spoon, directing it towards the food, scooping up a mouthful, and putting the food into the mouth. Each step is taught and each success is rewarded by praise and encouragement. Children with quite severe handicaps can be encouraged to learn new skills over a period of time by this method, or to modify their unacceptable and anti-social behaviour. The eventual goal is that of improving the child's overall performance within certain limits, according to the nature and severity of the child's handicap(s).

Some psychologists have also been concerned to teach parents behaviour modification methods to use with their behaviourally disturbed (but not physically of mentally handicapped) children. Parents are taught to use a system of rewards with their children, based on a carefully structured programme, to help the child overcome such problems as bed-wetting, temper tantrums or disobedience (see e.g. Herbert, 1981). Rather different 'partnership with parents' schemes have also been used on a larger scale. The best examples of this are probably those schemes where parents are involved in helping their children to read. Some of these schemes are relatively unstructured and the parent is merely encouraged to listen to the child at intervals (see Tizard *et al.*, 1982). Others are more structured, and based on certain specific techniques. Perhaps the most well-documented of structured schemes is that of 'paired-reading' (Morgan and Lyon, 1979; Bushell *et al.*, 1982). Here, the parent and the child read in unison until the child feels able to read on his own. The parent is given relatively precise instructions on how to read with the child, when to stop, and how to help the child if he cannot continue or manage a particular word.

Partnership between parents and psychologists has many possibilities, and it seems likely that psychologists will continue to develop and expand their ideas on the subject. It must, however, be said that some doubts have been expressed about some of the schemes. For example, Peter and Helen Mittler (1983) suggest that there is no real evidence to support the view that parental involvement in partnership schemes to help their mentally handicapped children actually improves the child's performance. Luterman (1979), discussing counselling the parents of deaf children, writes of the 'frenzied dedication' which some parents bring to the task of helping their children speak. Such over-involvement may, Luterman suggests, arise from feelings of guilt and despair in the parents, and result in an unhelpful over-pressurizing of the child. Gregory (1982) clearly describes the gap which exists between our knowledge of what deaf children appear to need (in terms of language input and intellectual stimulation), and the ways to apply that knowledge effectively. She suggests that it is possible to make interventions, based in good faith on certain psychological models, which may actually be harmful or counter-productive in their effects. She suggests, for example, that it is possible for the parent–child interaction to become too parent-centred, as the adult strives to follow certain instructions. The child's own efforts can therefore easily be missed or swamped. Featherstone (1981), writing as a parent of a handicapped child, makes the point that it is essential to take into consideration the emotional and physical stress which is placed on the whole family when one of its members is handicapped. Schemes to help the child must be able to take these stress factors into consideration.

There is perhaps a tendency to assume that parents are both able and willing to co-operate usefully with the psychologist simply because they say they want to help. The *desire* to help must be almost universal among parents who see their children in need of their assistance. But it cannot necessarily be assumed that this desire can always be usefully and effectively channelled to the child's benefit. Applying certain techniques on a regular basis can place a burden on parents who may already be burdened by other worries: financial or personal. For some parents, teaching certain skills to their handicapped child might be a pleasure; for others a real imposition. It might not, however, always be readily apparent which parent comes into which category.

Parents almost invariably feel guilt at their child's handicap, whatever its nature. If the handicap is of a fundamental and physical nature, the parents will almost certainly feel, however inappropriately, that they were somehow to blame. Feelings of guilt are inevitable, and parents may feel obliged to become involved in schemes to help their child overcome the handicap. Yet many of these schemes will be time-consuming, exhausting and with relatively little to show for a great deal of effort in terms of improvement in the child's behaviour and performance.

From the child's point of view, the position may be equally complicated. Children usually do their best to live up to parental expectations. Nevertheless, the child's feelings for the parents are often ambivalent. They love them naturally but may, equally, find them annoying, unreasonable, anxious or confusing from time to time. Equally, they may become depressed or disheartened if they have the impression that they are failing to match up to parental expectations.

These comments refer primarily to the structured partnership schemes where parents are involved over a long period in trying to improve the performance of their handicapped child. However, I would suggest that certain doubts also need to be expressed about partnership schemes which require parents to use certain behaviour modification techniques to improve the behaviour of their 'disturbed' or 'difficult' children (i.e. those who are not mentally or physically handicapped). This topic has received much less coverage than other partnership schemes. Douglas (1981) suggests that there may be certain problems within a family, or between members of the family, which operate against (parental) compliance with advice from the psychologist on ways to help their child. She suggests that the parents can only usefully be involved in schemes where they are required to use behavioural techniques to modify their child's behaviour if the psychologist also works with an understanding of the nature of the particular family system.

It seems likely that the success or failure of partnership schemes hinges on certain factors which may be difficult to quantify. The nature of the child's problem must be important. Some handicaps or problems are obviously easier to overcome than others. Family factors are equally as important, however, including stress factors, the parent–child relationship and the relationship between other family members. Almost equally important, perhaps, is the quality of the parent–psychologist and parent–teacher relationship, and the support for parents which is built into the scheme. Schemes which have a support-system for the parents seem more likely to succeed than those where the parent is left to struggle alone. Many schools are beginning to recognize the need for continuing parental support, and teachers are often willing to listen to parents when the need arises, as well as offering instruction and advice. Parents of severely handicapped children usually have their own support-groups with which psychologists may also be connected (see Pugh, 1982).

It is probable that parents will be more effective partners if they have the opportunity to discuss their more negative feelings about their child and about the scheme with the psychologist. It needs to be recognized, openly, that parents take on a commitment that can often be a burden when they undertake to help their child by using regular and specific techniques. They may be willing to do so, but at the same time need the opportunity to discuss their feelings of guilt, irritation and occasional despair with others. The parent who can be helped to feel that his more negative attitudes are normal, will probably be able to offer more effective help to the child.

It is, however, somewhat unrealistic to discuss all partnership schemes under one heading as though they were comparable with each other in method and in purpose. They vary greatly. There is a considerable difference between schemes which encourage parental co-operation in an informal manner (e.g. listening to their children read) and schemes which are based on parents learning and following detailed instructions. It is possible that the more detailed and structured a particular scheme is, the more difficult it may be for a parent to carry it out effectively. On the other hand, it is arguable that very relaxed and unstructured schemes may seem insufficiently important or effective to the parents to encourage their co-operation and long-term commitment. Perhaps the ideal scheme is one which has a relatively simple structure, and is backed up by considerable support for the parents from support-groups, counselling and family therapy.

Partnership schemes are relatively new, and it seems likely they will continue to grow and develop. The potential for such schemes is considerable, but they need to be based on a realistic understanding of certain family processes, and of the parent–child relationship. In a later chapter, this is discussed more fully with reference to certain case-histories.

5

Family therapy

At first sight, family therapy may appear to have little in common either with consultation or with the partnership models described in Chapter 4. A treatment method associated at present more readily with psychiatry than with educational psychology, family therapy is based on the concept that disordered or troubled behaviour in an individual can frequently be found to reflect unsatisfactory patterns of behaviour in the family as a whole. The therapist (psychiatrist, psychologist, social worker) therefore aims to promote change in the whole family, rather than focusing on the symptomatic member of the family (i.e. the referred patient, or client).

The family therapy movement is relatively new, and owes its success to a small group of people who have found the technique effective, and have written about and expanded their ideas on the subject. The rationale for the technique comes from two unrelated sources: psychoanalysis and systems theory (GST). Psychoanalysis contributes to family therapy an understanding of individual personality development and of the ways in which adult personality characteristics may affect children of the family, while systems theory describes the way in which transactions between individuals tend to be repeated in a circular manner, and are relatively predictable and self-regulating (see below).

Family therapists always describe the family as a system, although they vary greatly in the emphasis they place on the need to consider the personalities of individual members of the family, and the past events in the family's shared life-experience in addition to this. It is recognized, however, that there is no real conflict between considering family interactions in systems terms, and understanding the personality of individual members of the family (see Walrond-Skinner, 1976).

Recent models of family therapy, while not necessarily denying the concept of a 'disordered' family system, have tended to move towards the concept of a family in transition, or a family under stress. Symptomatic behaviour in one member of the family is therefore attributed to difficulties of adaptation (e.g. from childhood to adolescence), or to stress factors such as divorce, separation or death in the family.

The family as a system

The word 'system' is used to describe a collection of continually interacting parts which together make a whole that is more than the sum of those parts. There is a tendency for each part to affect, and in turn be affected by, all the other parts in the system. A kind of circular balance prevails: A affects B affects C which affects A. Once in motion, the patterns of the system tend to repeat themselves, and to maintain themselves constantly.

Perhaps the most simple example of a social system involving child and parent is one where the child always performs a certain act disliked by the parent (staying in bed late in the morning) and the parent always responds by nagging the child to no avail. The more the child resists the parent, the more the parent nags; the more the parent nags, the more the child resists the parent. There is deadlock between the two. Another example includes both parents and child. Mother and adolescent daughter regularly quarrel about the fact that the daughter is always going out. At a certain point, mother bursts into tears and father shouts: 'Don't shout at your mother!' Daughter says: 'You always side with her,' and rushes out of the house. The system serves the purpose of getting the daughter out of the house – but at the cost of a good deal of anger, anxiety and unhappiness in all members of the family.

In both these cases it is possible for the participants to act differently, but they fail to do so. (Father could, for example, step in earlier in the argument.) They are caught up in a system which seems to be stronger than the individual participants in the system. The reasons for this are not always easy to understand, but the tendency on the whole is for family patterns to be anxiety-reducing and/or rewarding to certain family members who therefore have an interest in perpetuating them. They are also taken for granted as being the right, or the only, way of behaving. There is a tendency for the patterns to have their roots in the early lives of the parents of the family. Returning to the example given above, it may be that the father of the daughter who always argues with her mother has anxieties about conflict with women which date back to his own childhood experience with a very powerful mother. He is therefore unable to step in and discipline his daughter in a straightforward way early in the proceedings, but lets the conflict rage until he can bear it no longer and then shouts: 'Don't shout at your mother' – with predictable results.

Family therapists are concerned to look at the way in which a particular family functions as a system, taking into consideration the actions and communications of all family members, and the contribution which these actions and communications make to the family's corporate being. However, therapists elaborate the relatively simple systems theory according to their own philosophies and theories.

The contribution of the psychoanalytic movement

The treating of whole families, in the case of behavioural disturbance in a child, was a natural development of traditional child guidance work, psychoanalytically based. Ackerman (1958) was one of the first to interpret the child's behavioural disturbance in terms of a 'disordered interplay' between family members and to interview whole families when treating a disturbed child. He suggested that different disorders within the family dynamics lead to pressure on the child who may react in one of three ways:

(1) by attacking the family by showing signs of behavioural (conduct) disorder
(2) by withdrawing and becoming preoccupied with himself and his body
(3) by showing signs of excessive anxiety and internalization of conflict Ackerman (1966).

Disorders of the family system, in psychoanalytical terms, originate in the past lives of parents and grandparents, and are related to interpersonal and intra-psychic conflict. These processes are largely unconscious, but they are held to have an important effect on behaviour. Oedipal conflicts, male/female rivalry and sibling rivalry are all held to have an important effect on human behaviour, and on the nature of the particular family system (Skynner 1976a).

Object-relations theory, based on the works of Melanie Klein, describes how the child's experience of his parents during the early years of life affects his relationship with others, including his spouse (see Scharff, 1982). This experience can also affect the way in which the individual responds to his or her own children. Thus parents who see their own parents as 'ideal objects' (rather than real people with human weaknesses) may have difficulty in recognizing and tolerating weaknesses in themselves or in their children.

Klein's theory of *projective identification* is also used. This suggests that the baby projects his angry feelings onto the mother, and then perceives the mother as attacking *him* as a result. Lieberman (1980) describes how this theory explains the way in which certain family patterns of 'pathological' behaviour may be passed from generation to generation. Theories of *interlocking pathology*, where some family members appear to carry feelings (e.g. of depression) on behalf of others, or to project their feelings into other members of the family are similar, and are regularly used by family therapists (see Walrond-Skinner, 1976).

Many family therapists who do not make much apparent use of psychoanalytic theory in their practice still openly recognize the debt they owe to the pyscho-analytic movement (Palazzoli *et al.*, 1978). It is not necessary to understand or to subscribe in full to the detail of this theory to be able to appreciate its value and relevance when helping families (Walrond-Skinner, 1976).

Other influences in the field of family therapy

The concept of deviant communication between family members

It is suggested that some parents have ways of communicating with their children which are confusing and potentially psychologically damaging to the child. There are two main influences in this field. Bateson *et al.* (1956) described the 'double-bind' communication used by parents with their children, in which two orders are given, one of which contradicts the other. The example Bateson gives is that of the parent who says to the child, 'Go to bed, you're tired', when the child is *not* tired. The message appears to be for the child's benefit, though it actually means that the parent wants the child out of the way. The child is confused. He knows he is not tired, but to say so is to contradict a statement apparently made for his benefit, and to recognize that the parent might want to be rid of him. Bateson suggests that he 'prefers' to accept the message that he is tired, thus falsifying his own, true feelings.

The parent appears to use the double-bind as a method of bringing about behavioural changes in the child without arousing his anger. The message is: 'Do as I say, but don't be angry with me (or reject me) for asking it.'

Laing and Esterson (1970) describe pathological patterns of behaviour in families, and deviant communication between parent and child, in a slightly different manner. They suggest that some parents perpetually deny the child's own thoughts and feelings, and attribute *their* thoughts and feelings to the child. Thus no one ever recognizes the child's right to have a separate viewpoint, and feelings of his own. The unwritten message is: 'Think and feel as I tell you that you think and feel, not as you really think and feel.'

Doane (1978), reviewing literature from studies concerned with the relationship between family patterns of behaviour and schizophrenic disturbance in one of the offspring, concluded that deviant communication was a reliable instrument for discriminating parents of offspring with thought disorder. There have unfortunately been few attempts made to relate behavioural disturbance in *children* with deviant parental communication, but Bugental *et al.* (1971) showed that a high proportion of parents of a group of children with behavioural difficulties at school produced conflicting messages in their communications with their children.

Structural family therapy

Structural family therapy is described as a 'body of theory and techniques that approaches the individual in his social context' (Minuchin, 1974). The focus of attention is on the way in which the particular family is organized. This includes a consideration of the hierarchical structure of the family (e.g. who is taking on the 'parent' role) and the alliances that take place between family members. 'Normal' families consist of a parental alliance, with the children as a separate sub-group:

[Mother + Father]

Daughter Son Daughter

When the family hierarchy is disturbed, the following position may exist:

[Mother + Son] Father

Daughter Daughter

or perhaps:

[Father + Daughter] [Mother + Son]

Daughter

Structural family therapists place emphasis on the importance of transactions that take place within the family. These transactions include both actions and words, and represent the rules of the 'game' of the particular family. They arise out of, and are designed to maintain, the family's structure and its different alliances. Although the origin of the transactions is usually lost, they have become an important part of the family's life in common and are maintained because of the moral and emotional components that accompany the transactions. They tend to be highly rewarding to (some) individual family members – though potentially damaging to others. A fundamental purpose of the different transactions of pattern within the family appears to be that of maintaining the family's belief system (that is to say, its view of itself and of the world): 'We do it this way' is the message. And, of individual members: 'So-and-so is always like that. He/she is the clever one/bad one/mummy's girl/etc.'

Another important concept of the structural family therapy school is that of boundaries between family members. Minuchin suggests that in disturbed families, members tend either to be too involved with each other, or too detached and remote. In other words, boundaries are either blurred, or too rigid. Natural, appropriate boundaries should exist between individuals and between generations. Parents need to be confident enough to play the parenting role without becoming child-like, or demanding too great a degree of maturity from the children. There needs to be a natural boundary between the adult couple and the children. Children need access to parents, but must be excluded from certain adult activities, and learn that certain things are not for them. And each individual member of the family needs to be able to respect the rights and feelings of other family members within this natural hierarchy.

Strategic family therapy

Strategic family therapy is described as any therapy in which the clinician designs his intervention to fit the problem (Haley, 1978). The therapist focuses on the problem (e.g. bed-wetting, school refusal) and on the transactions between family members who are connected with the problem. The underlying assumption is that the family's attempted solution of the problem is, in fact, the very thing which is maintaining it. The intervention by the therapist is designed to achieve some change in the communications (interactions) between family members which surround the problem, in the expectation that this will result in a diminution or disappearance of the symptom(s). Sometimes the intervention is based on direct communication with the family of the way in which the therapist sees the problem; at other times, it is based on a paradoxical communication (see Watzlawick *et al.*, 1968; Watzlawick, 1978).

One advantage of strategic family therapy is that it allows the therapist to work with part-families (e.g. mother and child), and to put to one side a consideration of the structure of the whole family, or any underlying dynamic processes. It would, however, be wrong to think that this school of thought ignores completely the nature of the whole family system. Haley (1978) suggests that when one member of the family is disturbed it can very often be shown that there is a confused hierarchical structure in the family as a whole. Although he may choose to focus on (say) the mother–son relationship on a bed-wetting problem, the therapist does not ignore the part played by the father in the family system, whatever that part might be.

Systemic family therapy

Although all family therapists make use of the understanding of a family as a system, Systemic family therapists (otherwise known as the Milan school) pay particular attention to the family system, and to the transactions between family members which create, reflect and maintain the system. This school of thought draws on theories of human communication (see Bateson *et al.*, 1956; Watzlawick *et al.*, 1968). The suggestion is that in certain families (i.e. those which are likely to need help for one of their members) there is a rigidity of communication between family members, designed to preserve sameness within the family, and to protect its particular view of the world. Thus communications tend to inhibit the growth and development of certain family members, particularly the children (see Palazzoli *et al.*, 1978). Systemic family therapists have designed a system of circular questioning which allows the therapist to challenge the family's belief system, and to open up areas of communication which have been left untouched by the family (see Campbell *et al.*, 1983).

A life-cycle, or trans-generational framework for family therapy

This approach to working with families, described by Carter and McGoldrick (1980) focuses on the concept of the family 'in transition' through the natural life-cycle. Individuals continually grow and change, and their needs, and the responsibilities placed on them, also change throughout their lives. Each individual must be able to adapt to each new stage of life: adolescence, child-bearing period, old age, etc. Similarly, each family needs to be able to make adaptations to allow for these natural changes in family members. It is suggested that some families lack the ability to adapt, and that it is these families which may show signs of stress when faced with a new situation (e.g. a child starting school or leaving home; the death of a grandparent). In addition to this, Carter and McGoldrick describe the stress factors which can occur outside the family system, placing pressure on a family which is already stressed as the result of within-family processes. Disturbed or deviant behaviour in a family member can arise from a combination of external and internal (within family) stress factors (see also Lieberman, 1980).

A Piagetian framework

This model has received relatively little attention in family therapy. However, the concept of a child adapting to the family environment, as he adapts to any other environment, is useful to educational psychologists who may be presumed to have a good understanding of Piagetian theory and terminology. Parental attitudes are assimilated, while the child at the same time accommodates to them. Where parental attitudes are clear, caring and reasonable, the child has little difficulty in the process of assimilation and accommodation. When they are unclear, confusing – uncaring even – the child has difficulty in doing so without inner conflict and loss of self-esteem, or without losing touch with reality. The child's behaviour may then become confused, erratic or angry often to the bewilderment of parents who are doing their best to help the child (French, 1977).

This is a very brief summary of some of the influences in the field of family therapy. They should not, however, be considered as separate from each other, since therapists almost invariably develop a method of intervention which is based on more than one of the models described. Certain concepts tend to recur continually in family work, and can be regarded as fundamental to an understanding of family systems and processes. The more important of these concepts, in summary, are:

(1) The family can be considered as a system, with the actions and attitudes of each member of the family affecting, and being affected by, other members of the family. These actions and attitudes have their roots in the past lives of family members, and in those of preceding generations.

(2) In certain families (e.g. those where one member of the family shows signs of disturbed behaviour) there may be a tendency for:

   (a) family members to take up, or be forced into, 'roles' which they may not want to play (they may be highly damaging) but which they paradoxically take for granted. These roles, played out and maintained in a system of interaction between family members, create and maintain the family's view of itself, its members, and of others outside the family system. Thus the family tends to create its scapegoat, its 'dependent' member, its 'difficult' member. Similarly, the family creates a view of the outside world (hostile, for example, or ready to be cheated or manipulated) and of itself (perfect, perhaps, or always in trouble).

   (b) the family's world view, and the roles of family members, are maintained by dysfunctional communication between family members (Satir, 1967). That is to say, the relationship between family members and their ways of being are continually reinforced by these dysfunctional communications. Thus a child is kept in a dependent/passive role by being told he cannot manage for himself. Or, an aggressive child is kept that way by being told he is like his (aggressive) uncle. In addition to this, some messages are extremely confusing to the child, who may be told to 'go away and grow up' at one moment, and 'if you leave me you'll upset me' at the next.

Dysfunctional communication appears to be emotionally satisfying to some or all family members. It also serves the purpose of avoiding real communication since this recognizes differences, weakness, pain or loss.

(c) natural hierarchies/boundaries/sex roles tend to be blurred. Adults tend to make unreasonable emotional demands of their children and/or promote them to adult status. Thus, a child is over-protected at one moment, and required to take unreasonable responsibility for himself and others at the next. Children sometimes get caught up in an inappropriate partnership with a parent (e.g. required to fulfil an adult role in the absence, say, of a father).

(d) the family has become 'stuck' in ways of behaving which might have been appropriate at an earlier stage in the family's life-cycle, but are no longer so. Thus parents may tend to hold on to their offspring, rather than encourage them to seek a more mature way of behaving. They appear unable to adapt their parenting to take account of the changing needs of their offspring, and the changing circumstances in their own lives.

Overall, the picture is one of a family system which is relatively rigid and stuck in its ways of behaving which are taken for granted by family members, though they may be highly detrimental to one or other person in the family. The reason for this state of affairs is complex, and readers interested in family therapy will want to read more widely on the subject. It is, however, important to remember that people are almost invariably unaware of the patterns and interactions in their own families, and of the ways in which some family members might be trapped into deleterious roles. They take themselves and their actions and attitudes for granted. They are caught up in a 'dance', made up of a sequence of steps which cannot be changed without the intervention of someone outside their system. The intervention needs to be based on a real understanding of the system, and of the part played in the system by each family member.

The family therapy movement is not without its critics. People have objected to the concept of 'psychopathology' (of individuals and of families) when applied in a rather sweeping manner to any family with a problem. The objection to such labelling is understandable, and therapists usually avoid it whenever possible. Certain techniques of intervention have also been criticized as being intrusive or manipulative of family members. There is also some controversy about which families can or should be helped in this way.

Psychologists or psychiatrists who prefer to use a therapeutic technique which is directed at the individual in his own right (e.g. medication, behaviour modification, individual psychotherapy) are sometimes impatient of the suggestion that the problem needs to be interpreted as part of a wider social context. There is conflict, too, between those professionals who think in terms of linear causality, and those who think in systems terms. There is some confusion and argument about what actually happens in family therapy. Therapists claim to know their own models and methods of intervention, and to defend them against the models and methods of others. The nature of change in families, and the reasons for lack of change in some families, are not always clear, nor is there a clear line to be drawn between supporting or working with a family, and family therapy.

Family therapy and the school psychological services

Family therapy is now widely used in a clinical setting, but it has, at the time of writing, made relatively little impact in the school psychological services. Although a substantial number of children referred to educational psychologists (even the *majority* of children) are referred with behavioural disturbance, help for the child is usually offered in the setting of the school system, rather than by involving the family in family therapy. This approach is obviously valuable (see e.g. Kolvin *et al.*, 1981), and it is not suggested that it can, or should be, replaced by family therapy. Nevertheless, family therapy could probably be used much more extensively than it is at present by educational psychologists, with advantage to many referred children.

There must be several reasons for the relative lack of enthusiasm shown by most educational psychologists for family therapy. In the first place, it is itself a relatively new technique. More important, perhaps, it tends in some measure to contradict the specific-condition models which form, or have formed, the foundation for the discipline of educational psychology. Carter and McGoldrick (1980) suggest that it comes naturally to think in terms of personality characteristics, or symptoms, as located within the individual concerned, and that it is difficult to move from this frame of reference to one which describes the individual in terms of the systems which include the individual. Educational psychologists have made the shift in one sense, by focusing increasingly on schools systems and decreasingly on the individual child, and it seems likely that they will also show an increasing interest in family systems. (The shift in the frame of reference is not, of course, only a problem for psychologists. In the field of psychiatry, for example, there is considerable controversy between those who focus on treatment of the individual, and those who are concerned with the family system.)

Educational pyschologists may also be reluctant to study the techniques of family therapy if they have had valuable experiences involving parents in partnership schemes. It may seem inappropriate, even unethical, to think of parents as clients, as a family therapist might. Yet this is surely to confuse two issues. There is a distinction between taking a detached look at a family system in an attempt to locate areas of difficulty for individuals in that system, and regarding parents as 'needing treatment'. It is undeniably the case that most parents want to do the best for their children. At the same time, many family systems are, or have been, under stress for one reason or another, and this stress can be harmful to a child in ways the parents may not always be aware of.

Although it seems likely that family therapy has considerable potential for helping behaviourally disturbed children referred to the school psychological services, it has never (as far as I am aware) been researched in that area. My own evaluation (Campion, 1984), although not a controlled research project, suggests that it is useful. Willan and Hugman (1982) also report favourably on the use of the technique in the school psychological services. Kolvin *et al.* (1981) refer to parent counselling as one of the possible techniques for helping children who show signs of behavioural disturbance at school, but this is not the same as family therapy, and probably less effective, since it does not involve the child himself.

It is suggested that an understanding of family systems, and of certain family therapy principles and techniques, has a purpose and a value which extends beyond using family therapy in its usually accepted sense. That is to say, it is always useful to try to interpret a child's behaviour, and to understand his general lack of progress at school, in terms of his experiences within his own family system. This understanding increases the psychologist's ability to help the child, regardless of the nature of the child's apparent difficulties.

6

The child's 'symptoms' and the family system

Most models of the parent–psychologist relationship appear to be based on the assumption that the child's unsatisfactory or immature behaviour, or his learning difficulties, are a facet of his own personality and intellect. In short, that there is 'something wrong with' the referred child which must be explained, treated or remediated. There is, therefore, an expectation that the psychologist will give the parents factual information, and make concrete suggestions for helping the child. If the parents are eventually co-opted as partners with the psychologist to help the child, there is still the feeling that the problem belongs to the child. In other words, in both the consultation and partnership models of the parent–psychologist relationship adults conspire to discuss the child and his problems as though others had no part in them; and parents are treated as though they were relatively detached from, and uninvolved with, the child in a social and emotional sense.

The family therapy model, on the other hand, is based on a different understanding of human behaviour and experience. Family therapists hold that the behaviour of an individual can never be considered in isolation and without reference to the behaviour and attitudes of other members of the family; they also suggest that past events have a powerful effect on the present behaviour of family members. In the case of children, the focus is never on the child alone or on his 'condition' or behaviour, but always on the actions and interactions of all members of the child's family, and on the shared life-experiences of family members.

It could be argued that the two approaches are so different that they are applicable to totally different situations – that is, it is, or should be, clear when a problem lies within the child, and when it is within the system. In some cases this appears to be so. For example, a child with a hearing loss has a problem of his own, whereas a behaviourally disturbed child might well be reacting to a troubled family system. On the other hand, the way in which the members of the family of the child with a hearing loss behave towards him, and react to his actions and communications, will have a profound effect on his general development. Unsatisfactory factors in the family system may, in fact, be a greater source of stress or handicap for the child than the hearing loss itself.

It is suggested that it is always worth considering that there could be a relationship between the child's 'symptoms' – regardless of their nature – and the family system. This suggestion might seem more obvious, and is perhaps easier to defend, in some situations than others. It is not uncommon to meet the parents of a referred child and to be aware that their attitudes have contributed significantly – though usually inadvertently – to the child's difficulties. But this is by no means always the case. In many instances, it is quite hard to see how the child's behaviour and performance are related to family processes. Yet the search for this relationship is nearly always worthwhile, and can, of course, always be abandoned if found to be unhelpful.

Possible relationships between the child's 'symptoms' and his experience within his own family system can usefully be considered under separate headings, as follows.

The child as part of a troubled family system

It is suggested that some family systems are, for one reason or another, more helpful to some children than others. Parental attitudes are important in creating for the child an environment in which he can flourish (see Chapter 7). Where these attitudes are reasonably stable, affectionate and mature, the child usually has little difficulty in developing a sense of self-respect and self-discipline. He knows what is expected of him, and has an inner sense of well-being which allows him to negotiate the more difficult aspects of life (e.g. separating from his parents at the start of schooling, changing schools, contact with new (perhaps stern) teachers, new experiences and new friendships). Such a child is usually able to make the most of what is available to him in the education system and even more important – to make stable relationships with others outside the family system.

However, where the family system reflects parental attitudes which, though well-meaning, are immature, anxious, confused, unreasonable or rigid, the child is much less able to understand what is expected of him and to develop a sense of his own competence. He tends not to have the inner sense of security and self-respect which allows him to respond positively to new and stimulating situations, or to adapt to difficult ones. He may be tense, restless, anxious and confused, and may react in an inappropriate manner (even perhaps violently) when faced with a new or stressful situation.

It is also suggested that, in many cases, although parental attitudes are adequate, and the family system basically sound, stress factors may have contributed to, or created, difficulties for the child. Children who have known confusing or painful domestic circumstances may continue to experience stress long after the parents have adapted to the changed circumstances. Indeed, a divorce or a separation may be a great relief to the adults, but leave the child confused and unhappy. Although many children appear to adapt remarkably well to changed domestic circumstances, others show signs of depression, lack of concentration in school and behavioural disturbance long after the event. It may not necessarily be the event itself which is the cause of the child's difficulties, however, but perhaps the child's confusion and lack of understanding of the situation. Alternatively, the child may have to cope with complex sharing or visiting arrangements, step-parents, or disagreements between parents. It is hardly surprising if a child living in such a situation has difficulty in learning, in concentrating at school, or in inhibiting his more anti-social attitudes.

The child's symptoms (observed at school) as an expression of the role he plays in the family system

It is suggested that many children, for many different reasons, take up (or are allocated) roles which have a function within the family system. A child who has been, perhaps unwittingly, encouraged to see himself as the 'bad' one at home, may carry his difficult behaviour directly into school. Equally, a child who feels that he is required to be good, passive and docile may well carry this behaviour into school, to the detriment of his natural enthusiasm and drive. A child may feel that he is required to act out certain behaviour on behalf of the parent – succeed, perhaps, where his father has failed; or be a spokesman for certain parental attitudes. He might feel himself required to take on an adult (parental) role *vis-à-vis* his brothers and sisters, so that he is continually involved in fighting their battles. Children who feel themselves 'on a level' with adults as a result of taking over a parental role at home may find it difficult to accept teachers' discipline at school.

The school-refusing child may sense her mother's depression and feel the need to stay at home to support her. A depressed child may have suppressed his own needs over a period of time to fit into complex marital arrangements which are more satisfactory to the adults than to the child.

Some children seem to feel the need to act as a peacemaker or to act as a bridge between warring or separating adults.

They may develop certain techniques for maintaining the *status quo* in the family – techniques which have a powerful effect on the child's behaviour and performance. The following example is of a boy whose reading difficulties seemed to be – at least partly – related to factors in his family system, and to his own need to be a bridge between his parents.

Robin, aged 9, was referred with a specific reading problem, diagnosed as dyslexia. He had had a considerable amount of private tuition for about two years, but was described as 'deteriorating' after initially making a very good start with the teacher. An investigation of the family background revealed that the parents had been living apart for a trial separation for about nine months – the period of time during which Robin had deteriorated. During this time the parents and Robin had come together again for a discussion of his reading. The father, who lived away from home, used to take Robin to his teacher twice a week, and called in at the home afterwards. In short, Robin had no real incentive to give up his symptom, since it provided the opportunity for bringing his parents together again. When his father moved away from the area and made a relationship with someone else, Robin began to read. Had this change in the system not happened spontaneously, the psychologist would have needed to consider the meaning of Robin's symptoms as part of the overall treatment plan to help him.

Sometimes the role a child feels required to play is helpful, at least up to a point. A child who feels bound to be the 'successful' one may, if he has the intellectual ability, do well at school. On the other hand, if he does not have the ability, and feels under heavy pressure to succeed, he may well show signs of strain or failure.

The child's symptoms and their relationship to adult anxiety

A child's symptoms (e.g. inability to read, speech problem, non-attendance at school) are often a source of considerable anxiety to parents, and sometimes a source of disagreement between them. It is unfortunately almost always true that parental anxiety leads to attitudes that are less than helpful to the child: sometimes too much pressure is put on a child; or parents may find themselves continually discussing, and arguing between themselves, about the best way of handling or treating the child. The child's symptoms, whatever their nature, tend to be increased by anxious, over-concerned parental attitudes. This increase in the child's symptoms tends to lead to a further increase in parental anxiety, creating an ever-increasing downward spiral, with parental attitudes becoming more and more inappropriate as the child's behaviour or performance deteriorates. Both sides need help to break out of the spiral.

It is suggested that parental anxiety almost always plays some part in maintaining the child's symptoms, and that this can be usefully considered as part of the total plan for helping the child. If the parents feel a little more relaxed and confident, it can frequently be demonstrated that the child's behaviour and performance begin to improve. It is, however, worth recognizing that parental anxiety may not be expressed openly, but more indirectly, for example in a tendency to blame others, or perhaps to move from one professional to another in the search for help and advice.

The family's resistance to change

In some cases a child's symptoms appear to be related to some degree of rigidity in the family system and to the parents' lack of ability to accept change and development in their children. Some parents cope admirably with their families when young, yet find it hard to adapt their style of parenting to meet the changing needs of their growing children. Equally, many children happily accept a close and rather restrictive family atmosphere when they are young, but rebel against it in adolescence. Thus it sometimes appears that two opposing forces motivate families:

the need for growth, development and change, and the desire for sameness, routine and predictability. Ideally, these forces should be in balance in a realistic, give-and-take manner. Occasionally, however, the system seems unable to adapt sufficiently to meet the changing needs of individual family members, and a child may become 'stuck' in a role which he no longer wants.

An example is that of the child who takes on a supportive role in the family (perhaps a parental role in the absence of one of the parents) willingly, until he reaches adolescence when the attractions of his peer group conflict with family demands. The child's growing need for independence, expressed perhaps in moody, 'difficult' behaviour and a refusal to carry out tasks which were previously undertaken quite readily, conflicts sharply with the family's view of him as helpful, co-operative and supportive. Family communications and attitudes, which are all based on the assumption that he will continue to play a supportive role, tend to break down. Family members become angry, depressed, confused. The child may take refuge in school refusal, or in negative or extravagant behaviour.

There are, of course, many other ways in which the tendency to be unable to adapt to change results in behavioural disturbance in the child. The birth of a baby may mean that older children must adapt to the fact that parents have less time for them. If this coincides with starting school for the older child, there could well be a period of difficult behaviour. Illness, handicap, death or divorce in the family all change the circumstances to which family members must adapt themselves. Some children can do this successfully, others show signs of stress.

The child's contribution to the family system

One of the advantages of systems theory is that it avoids labelling people as victims or aggressors and thereby attributing blame to one or other party. Each person is seen as making his unique contribution to the system (and in the case of families, to the *status quo* in a particular family). When parents shout or nag, their children resist by whatever way seems most appropriate to them, and there is a tendency for people to get stuck, unable to move towards more constructive ways of behaving towards each other.

It may be supposed that the resistance which children put up to their parents' well-meaning efforts to teach, discipline or control them arise from a number of different factors. A natural desire to test adult limits is an important factor; so, too, is the desire to protect their own self-esteem, and therefore to resist discipline which is seen as destructive or negative. Quite often, the child is genuinely confused as to what is expected of him by adults, and behaves accordingly. Roe (1978) speaks of the ways in which children 'dig holes' for themselves, with adults tending to keep them there – to the despair of all concerned – so that an unsatisfactory system comes into being.

To suggest that children make their own contribution to the family system is not to deny that they are, unfortunately, usually at greater risk than the adults in the system. They are sometimes physically and emotionally at risk in view of their relative weakness and dependency on the parents. Equally, and perhaps more often, they are at risk of acquiring ways of behaving which place them at a disadvantage *outside* the family system. Certain attitudes in the child may serve a purpose within the family system but, brought into school, can make life extremely difficult for him, and for others. Even more seriously, the child who lives in an unsatisfactory family system may find it difficult to create for himself a satisfactory family system of his own in adulthood. It is therefore important to recognize that, although the child appears to be playing his part in maintaining an unsatisfactory family system, he is – potentially at least – the loser.

Although the child's experience within his family system is a crucial factor in determining the way in which he behaves and performs at school, it is not always easy to see how the two are related. It is easy enough when the child behaves in a very similar manner at home and at school, but some children behave very differently in other environments. Even in these cases, however, there is quite often a link. A passive, quiet child in a tense family may find the challenge of school too much to bear: he is 'good' at home, hyperactive, moody and aggressive at school. Sometimes parental attitudes are so strict that children dare not misbehave at home, and so work out their frustrations at school. Sometimes, of course, children are difficult at home, but well-behaved and hard-working at school (these cases will not, of course, often be seen by educational psychologists).

Conclusion

I should like to return to the suggestion that there is often some relationship between the child's 'symptoms' and the family system which can usefully be understood by the psychologist as part of the overall procedure to help the child. It is hoped that it is clear by now that this does not imply that parents are at fault in the more usually accepted sense of this expression. Rather, that certain processes within the family system, or certain events in the family's life-history, have created (or are creating) some difficulties for the child – difficulties which need to be taken into consideration when involving the parents in an attempt to help their child.

I would suggest that it is occasionally clear to the psychologist that the child's behaviour reflects certain fairly obvious difficulties in the family system, and/or a relatively unsatisfactory parent–child relationship, and that family therapy therefore appears to be the treatment of choice. Alternatively, it may sometimes be clear that the parent–child relationship is good, and the family system stable, so that the psychologist can embark immediately on a scheme which involves the parents as partners (for example, in a paired-reading scheme).

In a certain number (perhaps the majority) of cases, however, it may not be immediately obvious why the child is in difficulties, or why he is making insufficient progress at school. The psychologist can then usefully stand back a little and allow herself time to consider the situation. She can show herself willing to listen to the parents, give them space to discuss their own fears and anxieties and encourage them to give certain information which should increase her understanding of the child and his difficulties. She can take a closer look at the family system, and at the interactions which may well take place between individuals during a family interview. In short, the psychologist can try to extend her knowledge and understanding of the child, not only as an individual but as part of his own, unique, family system. She can try to see how his symptoms might fit into, or reflect, the experiences, which he has had in the past and which he may continue to have in the present.

Listening to, and talking to both the child and his parents, the psychologist begins to understand them as individuals *and* as part of a system. Working with them over a period of time, it is possible to make use of this understanding, not only for the child's benefit, but often for the benefit of the whole family.

7

The family under stress

Surprisingly little attention has been paid to the family circumstances of children referred to the school psychological services. Educational psychologists have, for one reason or another, been somewhat reluctant to comment on the family background of the children they see. There is, therefore, little or no hard information on which to base a discussion of the important topic of stress factors in families of referred children.

There has, of course, been research on the relationship between certain adverse social factors (e.g. financial deprivation, poor housing, divorce) and lack of achievement in school or delinquent behaviour in young people (see e.g. Wedge and Prosser, 1973; Pilling and Kellmer-Pringle, 1978). However, there is no real link made between this type of research and the children who are referred to the school psychological services. It sometimes seems that we regard stress factors in a child's life as an *additional* burden for him to bear, rather than as having a fundamental influence on his total social, emotional and cognitive development. It is probably also true to say that research of this nature has concentrated largely on gross measures of family stress rather than on the more subtle factors of unsatisfactory interpersonal relationships.

Research in this area is notoriously difficult for many reasons. Some might even argue that the family circumstances of referred children are the responsibility of others (e.g. social workers) and not the concern of educational psychologists at all. Yet this cannot really be the case. Educational psychologists need to be concerned with the child's *total* development: social, emotional and cognitive. It is extremely difficult – if not impossible – to separate these aspects of the child's development; equally as difficult to consider them without considering the nature of the child's experience in his relationships with others (e.g. family members). It is suggested, therefore, that a consideration of stress factors in the family forms an important part of the diagnostic task, particularly if the psychologist wishes to involve the parents in helping a child. Before looking at some of these factors, attention is paid to the nature of the parental role, since it is against the background of Winnicott's 'good enough' parenting that stress within a family system needs to be considered.

Parents and the parental role

It hardly needs saying that the young of all species need adult figures to care for them, protect them and introduce them into the rules of the group or society in which they live. Although the process varies from species to species (and, in the case of human beings, from society to society) there are important common factors. The process starts with a close parent–child bond and with adult attitudes that are nurturing, accepting and containing of the very young infant. This is followed by a period in which the young gradually extend the range and scope of their activities. They move farther and farther away from the parent(s), returning from time to time for reassurance, food and protection, until they are ready to take full responsibility for their own lives, and to become parents in their turn.

Throughout the period of maximum growth and development, the young are continually both encouraged and controlled by parental actions and attitudes. With the welfare of their offspring at heart, parents shape and modify the behaviour of the young with appropriate signs of approval or disapproval. At the same time, adults are continually acting as models for their offspring. This dual process ensures that their young have a good chance of acquiring behaviour patterns which are both effective for survival, and acceptable to other members of the group.

Parenting, and the parental role, involves many different factors and processes, some easier to identify than others. Burton-White (1975) describes the primary functions of adult caretakers as designers (of the environment), consultants to their children, and authority figures. Parents are usually ready to accept their role as designers and consultants with enthusiasm, and much emphasis has recently been placed on the role of parents as facilitators or educators of their children. This has, on the whole, been a positive approach to parenting. However, adults who are hard-pressed to fulfil their children's basic needs to eat and keep warm, as well as paying some attention to their own needs, may feel burdened by the suggestion that they should supply intellectual stimulation as well.

But it is in the area of discipline that many parents experience real difficulties – indeed, the subject of discipline is a source of much anxiety, confusion and muddled thinking in society as a whole. On the one hand, there is a tendency to confuse confident and caring 'setting of limits' with concepts of punishment and control. On the other hand, some people find real difficulty in distinguishing between adult attitudes towards children which encourage independence and self-determination, and attitudes which give the child license to behave exactly as he wishes.

Gurman (1981) suggests that parents need certain personality attributes if they are to be able to fulfil the parental role successfully. Among these he speaks of the need for the parents to have a strong, well-differentiated sense of self, and realistic expectations both of each other and of their children. He suggests, too, that parents need to have separated emotionally from their own family of origin, so that the family of procreation can be put first. Parents who have achieved this level of adult identity and maturity are able to offer their children real warmth and affection while maintaining a suitable generation gap between themselves and their children. They are also able to tolerate and stand up to their children's occasional difficult, obstreperous behaviour without either being overwhelmed by it, or becoming too angry with the child.

Ackerman (1958) suggested that parents, as well as being reasonably mature individuals, need to be confident of their own sexual identity, otherwise they find it impossible to create a satisfactory emotional climate for the children, and equally impossible to offer the children the opportunity to develop a successful sexual identity of their own during adolescence and early adult life.

Skynner (1976b) suggests that we cannot be sure of the *essential* differences between the sexes: that is, those differences required for mental health, as distinct from the non-essential cultural variants. Though this topic is fraught with difficulties, it cannot be ignored. Psychologists working with adolescents will be well aware that many are confused as to their sexual identities. (This is also true of younger children, but less noticeable.) Some adolescents admit openly to this; others will indicate it in manner or appearance. For some, it may be a source of anxiety and even real unhappiness.

As children grow and develop, parents must be able to adapt their own parenting style to the changing needs of the children. The family itself should be able to grow, change and adapt to allow for the changing needs of family members (Carter and McGoldrick, 1980). The close-knit family suitable for young children must be allowed to spread and develop as children move outwards and away from the family centre. Parents should be able to love, and then to let go when the time comes (Jenkins, 1981).

This 'letting go' is applicable in different ways to children and parents of all ages and stages of development. Parents taking their children to school for the first time often feel the pain of separation more acutely than the child. Indeed, it is often *their* anxieties which are communicated to the child and result in school refusal. Parents of older children know the difficulty of coming to terms with the fact that children may want to take part in activities which are potentially hazardous. And the parents of young adults must adapt to the knowledge that their child no longer 'belongs' to them as he once did.

Physical growth and change in the child take place continually as the inner forces of maturation impel him towards adulthood and away from the family of origin. Environmental factors may facilitate, or distort, this natural process – but it has its own momentum. The goal for the child is that of achieving a clearly identified personality, well integrated and self-sufficient, successfully separated from the family of origin. The task for the parents is that of adapting themselves and their behaviour to these changes while maintaining their own individuality and their own adult relationship with each other.

In summary, it is suggested that parents need to be:

(1) adequate facilitators of the child's intellectual and social development
(2) reasonably secure in the adult role and in their separate sexual identities
(3) able to offer their children a reasonably realistic view of the world (their communications with their children therefore need to be clear, unambiguous and consistent)
(4) able to withstand the emotional pressures associated with child-rearing: to set sensible limits and to accept the child's occasional angry response.

Parents under stress

There are many factors in the lives of adults which place the individual, the couple, or the family as a whole under stress. These range from external factors such as poor housing and lack of money, to more complex factors associated with the personality of individuals and/or with interpersonal relationships. External factors are not within the scope of this book, but it is important to look briefly at some of the more subtle *personal* factors which can place a strain on parents or a family, and on the child. These include:

(1) normal stress factors associated with child rearing
(2) stress factors associated with life-events
(3) within-parent factors
(4) within-child factors.

Normal stress factors associated with child rearing

The parental task is a demanding one, which takes up at least twenty years of adult life, and can, for some, prove too great a burden to bear. Arguably, parents in western societies make heavy weather of what is, after all, a natural process. It may also be true to say that adults sometimes seem to want the pleasure of children, without having any real understanding of the responsibilities of child rearing.

Continued contact with children can be emotionally and physically tiring, even if immensely rewarding. Possibly the area of discipline is that which causes greatest anxiety among parents. Many people experience extreme difficulty in setting reasonable limits on their children's behaviour, particularly during adolescence. Indeed, this period is one that can be especially stressful for families. Parents who have coped more or less successfully with their young children may find themselves quite unable to cope with the testing of limits that is a natural part of adolescent behaviour, and tend to withdraw from the task completely, or perhaps react to the child's normal truculence or laziness with acute anxiety, anger and confusion. The parents' behaviour makes things difficult for the child, who may take refuge in behaviour which is even more undesirable.

The normal stress factors associated with child rearing are of course increased by other stress factors, outlined briefly below.

Stress factors associated with life-events

There are certain events within the life-cycle of the extended family which might be presumed to place family members under varying degrees of stress. These include: death of a parent, child or sibling; prolonged separation of child from parent; divorce/separation of parents; being adopted or fostered; being a member of a single-parent family; or long periods of illness and/or hospitalization.

Unhappy or tragic events within a family can have repercussions for many years, which might adversely affect some family members. A divorce or separation, with associated problems of access to the children, step-parenting, financial hardship, all place a strain on adults and children alike. Prolonged separation of parents from children (or one parent from the family) can be stressful; so, too, is the period of adaptation needed when the family is reunited. The death of a parent, or a child, miscarriage and stillbirth are all traumatic events which can result in distress and depression in one or more members of the family, with unhappy repercussions for others.

The exact relationship between a traumatic event in a family and behavioural disturbance in a family member is not easy to assess. Some children do seem to survive quite difficult and stressful periods in family life (divorce, for example), and it may well be that it is a combination of factors that prove damaging to children – for example, living with a mother who is depressed, *and* losing a father through a divorce. It may also be that the child's interpretation of the stressful event is particularly damaging to him (see Walczak and Burns, 1984). Children sometimes blame themselves, however inappropriately, for parental separation or for someone's death. Parents may not necessarily be aware of this, but the burden on the child can be considerable.

But it is possible to look closely at what is *apparently* the stress factor in a child's life and to ignore other factors which are more important. The following example can perhaps illustrate this point briefly.

M, aged 8, was referred to the school psychological service when she began to miss school following her parents' divorce. Although this was initially felt to be a reaction on the part of the child to the departure of her father, the situation was, in fact, more complicated. It became apparent, on closer investigation, that M's behaviour had been giving cause for concern intermittently for a number of years, though not quite to the point of warranting a referral. It was also apparent, during the interview with the mother and child, that the mother was quite seriously depressed following the breakdown of her marriage, and that she was exaggerating M's difficulty in attending school, keeping her away on the slightest pretext, and commenting that it was 'all the fault of the divorce' that M was refusing to go to school. The psychologist was given the impression that the mother was hoping to bring home to her departed husband 'what he had done to the family' by leaving. It also became apparent that the mother's attitude to the child was unsatisfactory in a more general sense – an older brother was also showing signs of delinquent behaviour. Family communications were somewhat deviant, and attitudes rigid and (on the mother's part) guilt-provoking.

It was felt, therefore, that the separation of the parents was only one part of a complicated pattern of behaviour within the family. Help for the child included a discussion of practical factors (e.g. visiting arrangements) as well as a sympathetic understanding of the differing viewpoints of family members. The mother's despair and anger were acknowledged, and she was offered sympathy and support. At the same time, the child was encouraged to feel that her own life could continue, in spite of the departure of the father.

Within-parent factors

The parents of some referred children have ways of behaving, or personality characteristics, which give the psychologist cause for concern. Some parents seem very vulnerable, deprived or immature. Others may be more noticeably disturbed: depressed, violent or alcoholic.

Unsatisfactory parental personality characteristics quite often reflect unhappy experiences in the parents' own early lives, representing adaptations which the parents have had to make, over a number of years, to enable them to cope with stress during their own childhood and adolescence. Quite often these adaptations are successful from the parents' point of view, but appear to prevent them from offering their children the mixture of warmth and discipline needed by the growing child.

Emotionally damaged or inadequate parents find it particularly hard to undertake the parental role. Their own needs are often overwhelming and unfulfilled, and they ask more from their children in terms of emotional support than is appropriate. It is not uncommon to find parents (particularly an unsupported mother) unwittingly using a child to fulfil their own emotional needs. Occasionally the child is kept as a baby by a well-meaning parent, rather than being encouraged to develop his own strengths and identity.

Parents with a very unsatisfactory background of their own may try to avoid all conflict with the child. He may be over-indulged, with parents giving him material goods, perhaps as a substitute for the real affection they feel unable to give. Similarly, they may give in to his slightest whim. Alternatively, they may go to the other extreme and administer harsh discipline for trivial offences. The cycle of emotional deprivation and damage continues, depressingly, from one generation to the next.

Parents with a difficult or unsatisfactory background sometimes worry too much about their children. As soon as there is the slightest difficulty they may assume that the child is destined to end up in 'trouble' – or even in prison – since this has happened to other family members. Such negative attitudes are, of course, extremely unhelpful to children and may in fact create the very problem which the parent apparently seeks to avoid.

Within-child factors

A child's personality is the result of a mixture of complex factors and processes dating back to the early years of life. Nature and nurture both play their part. Regardless of the reasons for certain personality characteristics in a child, it is undoubtedly the case that some children are easier to handle than others – some seem to have a relaxed, easy-going temperament, while others appear to create difficulties for their parents from a very early age.

Certain within-child factors are particularly hard to bear. Most difficult of all, of course, is physical or mental handicap. Children who cannot respond normally to an adult, or understand simple requests or suggestions as the result of physical damage or deficit, place a great strain on parents, even if they are also dearly loved. Parents faced with the knowledge that their child's handicap is both fundamental and permanent bear not only the burden of having to cope with and help the child, perhaps until their own death, but the additional burden of guilt, anger or despair. The repercussions on the rest of the family of living with a seriously handicapped child can be considerable: there is less parental time and energy available for siblings, who may feel, at times, neglected or resentful.

Other within-child factors of a more subtle nature may place the parents, and therefore the family as a whole, under strain.

A child who belongs to one of the spouses only (for whatever reason) may not necessarily be liked by the step-parent, for example. Some children, too, appear to have characteristics which remind an adult of a disliked relative, which may adversely affect the adult's attitude to the child.

Grandparents

Although the grandparents of a referred child will rarely be seen by the educational psychologist, their presence will often be felt – sometimes quite strongly – since they will have played an important part in creating present-day parental attitudes. If they live near the family, they may continue to influence the way in which the parents handle their growing children. Sometimes this influence is positive in that they may help with baby-sitting, offer good advice, or make financial contributions. At other times the influence is less positive.

It is impossible to engage here in a full discussion of the way in which grandparents might be both unhelpful and helpful in their attitudes towards younger members of the family, and a few comments must suffice. It is, for example, clear that sharing a home with an elderly relative can place a strain on all younger members of the family, even if the relative is dearly loved. At times it may be apparent that collusion is taking place between a grandparent and a grandchild against the parent – perhaps by giving pocket money against parental wishes.

Some adult children remain emotionally very dependent on their own parents (most commonly, perhaps, women on their mothers); others retain angry and resentful feelings about past events or occasions when they have felt slighted, rejected or neglected. Such ties with the past can make it difficult for an adult to move forward, and make relationships in their own marriage that are stable and satisfying. Parental attitudes to their own parents may be confused or ambivalent, and this confusion is passed on to the children. One young mother who had been rejected by her own mother and had never come to terms with her premature death, continued to speak of her mother in the present tense. But during a meeting with the psychologist she complained that her child was 'odd', because he did not seem to know that Gran had died!

8

Involving parents: the early stages

Since children are most commonly referred to the school psychological services by teachers (with parents' permission), it is the usual practice of most educational psychologists to see them at school. The child may be given an individual assessment by the psychologist, who will also want to discuss his behaviour and performance with his teachers. Parents may come to the school to meet the psychologist, or they may be invited to meet her at a later date elsewhere.

Although there are many ways of approaching the task of helping children with behavioural difficulties and/or learning problems, there are considerable advantages in inviting the parents to bring the child to meet the psychologist at her office, rather than at school, as soon as possible after the referral has been made. This gives the psychologist the opportunity of seeing the child in the company of his parents as well as seeing him alone. Not only does this allow her to gain valuable information about the child from the parents, but it also allows her to establish a positive relationship with them as part of the total process of helping the child. (The child's behaviour and performance at school can, of course, be discussed with teachers at a later date.)

Parents may well be more disposed to form a satisfactory relationship with the psychologist if they have brought the child for assessment themselves and have been given the opportunity to discuss his difficulties as *they* see them at an early stage in the proceedings. Occasionally, an early discussion – a clearing of the air with the child and his parents – can bring about a marked improvement in his behaviour at school so that further intervention becomes unnecessary. Even if this does not happen, it is always helpful to make contact with the child's parents as soon as possible, and to hear their views on the nature of the child's difficulties. A letter can be sent to the parents referring to the school's concern about the child and suggesting that the psychologist would like to meet the family and hear what they feel about the child's difficulties. Although this is not always successful, in most cases the parents' response is good in my experience.

Psychologists who work regularly with families in a clinical setting sometimes insist that the whole family attend a session designed to discuss the problems of an individual child. Valuable as it is to see the whole family, this approach seems inappropriate in the setting of a school psychological service. The psychologist has a duty to see a child who appears to be failing within the education system, and is not in a position to be too dogmatic about the way in which she works.

The child alone

Most psychologists would probably agree that it is important to see a referred child alone, as well as discussing him with others and/or observing him in the classroom. The *formal* psychological assessment of the child can be undertaken with parents present and indeed, sometimes ought to be made in the presence of the parents, particularly if the child is very young or handicapped. Furthermore, the 1981 Education Act gives parents the right to be present during the assessment if they wish. Nevertheless, most children benefit from a session with the psychologist alone, during which they can be given the opportunity to show their ability and to express themselves to an adult whose training allows her to understand child behaviour and development. Interestingly enough, very few parents object to this individual session: most seem to respect it, and recognize its value.

The formal assessment includes the use of a number of standardized tests – although the enthusiasm which was once felt for these has waned somewhat in recent years. They are useful in comparing a child's behaviour with that of others of the same age group, but less effective as a means of discovering the causes of a child's failure, or as a method of indicating the best way in which a child should be helped. (They have been well described and discussed elsewhere, and it is not proposed to describe them again here.) Most psychological assessments are valuable in that they are designed to throw light on the child's problems in many different ways. In addition to the standardized tests, they include techniques which can give the psychologist some insight into the child's inner world, and his experience of himself and of others since there is almost always some relationship between the child's inner experience and his observable behaviour, though this relationship may not always be easy to see. Psychologists therefore encourage children to talk, to play, to draw, and to fill in a sentence-completion test in an attempt to understand the child more fully. Some will also use certain well-recognized projective techniques (e.g. the Bene–Anthony test, or the Rorschach test).

The individual assessment is, of course, confidential. The psychologist keeps information offered by the child in mind, but does not convey it directly to the parents unless the child wishes it to be given.

The family session

The family session can take place before or after the individual session with the child. It is often useful just to see the family together for a fairly brief discussion of the child's problem, then for the individual session to take place, followed by a further meeting with child and parents, either on the same day or a week or so later. Much depends on the nature of the problem, the number of people who attend the interview, the time available to the psychologist, and so on.

The family session needs to take place in a relaxed setting where there are enough reasonably comfortable chairs for everyone, and some play material for the children if they are young. The psychologist introduces herself and greets each member of the family individually. She can then comment briefly on the reason for the referral as *she* sees it, and invite the parents and the child to comment on the reasons for the referral as *they* see it. (Sometimes a child can usefully be asked for *his* point of view at the very beginning of the interview.)

It is helpful for parents and child(ren) to hear the psychologist commenting on the child's difficulties in a straightforward and non-judgemental manner. The child should be accepted as he is, although it is assumed at the same time that he wants to overcome his difficulties, whatever they may be.

Family interviews as described by family therapists (e.g. Walrond-Skinner, 1976; Haley, 1978; Minuchin, 1974) can be usefully adapted for use in the setting of a school psychological service. Family therapists stress the importance of addressing each person individually by name from the opening of the interview. Each person answers for himself (unless very young), and is treated by the psychologist as having a valid viewpoint which is worth listening to. The family-therapy model of information-gathering is also useful. Information which the psychologist needs if the child's symptoms are to be understood is taken, little by little, during the course of conversation with the family, with the psychologist focusing on the information which seems to have some bearing on the child's experience and on his behaviour (Bentovim, 1979), and passing over less important information.

However, while educational psychologists can learn much from family therapists on the technique of family interviewing, there are important differences between working in a clinical setting and holding a family interview in the setting of the school psychological service. In the clinical setting, the parents can often see that the child's problem might be their concern; in the school psychological service, parents usually see the problem as school-based. Indeed, it might well turn out to *be* school-based, though the psychologist needs an open mind about this before she is in full possession of the facts. In short, although the techniques described by Waldron-Skinner, Haley and others are extremely valuable in engaging parents whatever the nature of the child's problems, the psychologist must also be aware of the educational dimension of the child's problems; for example, it is inappropriate to focus too intently on the parents and their actions and attitudes, unless the parents themselves express concern about the child's behaviour at home. If they *do* express this concern, the psychologist has a valuable opportunity to widen the area of discussion with the parents; if they do not, some caution is needed.

The psychologist needs to be aware that parents may be understandably nervous or uncertain during the initial interview. An angry, defensive manner may hide real anxiety about their child's behaviour or performance at school. The occasional interview can be very difficult. However, it is always important for parents to feel that their viewpoint has been given a fair hearing.

As far as the child is concerned, it is important to get his impression on the reasons for the referral, and for the visit to the psychologist. He should be asked directly about this, unless he is very young. It is also important for the child to feel that, whatever the nature of the referral, the psychologist understands that his viewpoint is separate from that of others, and has its own validity.

Although parents may communicate relatively freely about themselves to a sympathetic listener, they sometimes have doubts about discussing the child's difficulties in front of him.

Since a degree of openness is essential in family work, this needs to be overcome. If the psychologist shows by her manner that the child's difficulty is to be discussed openly by asking the child for his viewpoint, this is usually sufficient to encourage free conversation. If, for example, the child's poor reading, temper tantrums or bed-wetting is the topic of conversation, the psychologist can use the opportunity to sympathize with the child if that seems appropriate. It does tend to be forgotten that behaviour problems and learning difficulties are usually as hard for the child to bear as they are for everyone else – at least at one level.

Eliciting as much information as possible

It is part of the psychologist's task to elicit as much information about the child and the family as possible, while still maintaining a rapport with the parents. This can sometimes be done more easily with some families than with others, and will depend partly on the psychologist's skills at extracting information without sounding too inquisitive, and partly on the parents' ability/desire to talk about themselves and their child. The temptation to take notes while the parents talk is considerable, but it does interrupt the free flow of conversation. A compromise can be reached by the psychologist recording matters of fact (e.g. names, ages of children, schools attended) during the interview, and leaving more detailed comments and observations on the family to be recorded after the session.

The nature of the information needed by the psychologist from the parents as a part of the diagnostic procedure varies according to the apparent nature of the child's difficulties. If, for example, the psychologist suspects that the child is mentally handicapped, she will probably want quite detailed information about the child's early months of life, the perinatal period and the early developmental milestones. If the child does not appear to be mentally handicapped, but is showing signs of behavioural disturbance and/or learning difficulties, other information may be more important. In summary, the psychologist will probably seek some or all of the following information from the parents in greater or lesser detail:

early history and developmental milestones;
physical health of child, including periods of hospitalization;
health of parents (hospitalization, long-term illnesses);
any separation, divorce, fostering, step-parenting;
details of other members of the family (siblings, grandparents);
child's behaviour at home (activities, hobbies);
discipline problems at home (if any);
educational experience (e.g. changes of school).

This information cannot be gathered all at once without leaving the parents feeling bombarded by questions. Indeed, it is better gathered more gently, over a period of two or three sessions, and used as part of a total strategy for understanding and helping the child. This technique is well described by Bentovim (1978, 1979) for use in a clinical setting, and can easily be adapted for use in the setting of a school psychological service. (This is described in greater detail in Chapter 10.)

In addition to gathering information about the child, the psychologist can usefully enquire about the parents' own past lives and experiences, if this can be done without appearing inquisitive. It is helpful, for instance, to know how the parents felt about their own schooling, and these questions can be put when the subject of the child's behaviour at school comes under discussion. The parents' replies may indicate how their own experiences have, for better or worse, shaped their attitudes to their child's education. If a parent hated school, it may be the case that he has communicated the dislike of school and teachers to the child, with adverse effects on the child's behaviour at school. On the other hand, if the parent was highly successful at school, he may find it hard to sympathize with a child who finds school overwhelming and difficult, or to offer realistic encouragement to such a child.

It is also helpful for the psychologist to ask the parents if they remember being the referred child's age, and how it felt. Were they happy/unhappy, successful/unsuccessful? Such questions can lead to a fruitful sharing of experiences to the benefit of both child and parents. They are rarely seen as intrusive, although the psychologist needs to be able to judge sensitively when *not* to press a particular point.

Parental attitudes

It is important for the psychologist to accept the parental viewpoint as a genuine expression of their thoughts and feelings about the child and his difficulties (and, indeed, about any other topic). On the other hand, it is equally important to be aware that that viewpoint is probably only one facet of parental personalities and attitudes, and that other attitudes may be revealed during the course of further discussion. For example, the parents may not be willing to admit to their own anxieties about their child until they know the psychologist and, during the initial meeting they may insist that there is 'nothing wrong' with him, or that his behaviour and performance is the school's fault. Later, they may well communicate real anxiety to the psychologist about the child.

Quite often a good deal of confusion and anger is associated with the child's behaviour, particularly if he has been in trouble at school for disruptive behaviour, non-attendance, not doing his homework, and so on. Parents are understandably defensive of their children, yet their own attitudes quite often unfortunately contribute to the child's behavioural difficulties. It is for example sometimes possible to see that parents are sending conflicting messages to their child: 'Do as they tell you' versus 'Don't let them get one up on you'. It may also be clear at times that parents are very anxious about or dislike the school, and that the child has picked up his anti-school attitudes from them. (It is recognized that some anti-school attitudes are justified. The point is, however, that a child who constantly hears negative attitudes from his parents about schools and teachers cannot really be expected to adapt himself to any school regime.)

While some parents seek to deny that the child is ever difficult, or seek to blame the school, other parents may be quite genuinely confused about why teachers are worried about their child. This is particularly the case with children who have been referred for very passive, immature and withdrawn behaviour. The parents may see the child's excessive docility as both normal and desirable, and cannot understand that others are worried by it.

Parental attitudes towards the psychologist can be revealing. Some parents seek to excuse, to placate, to agree with everything that is said; others may try to dominate and control the psychologist. It is important to make allowances for the fact that the parents may feel ill at ease when talking to the psychologist. Nevertheless, the observations are important. It is not unreasonable to suppose that a father who tries to bully the female psychologist is also something of a bully elsewhere, or that a mother who sounds depressed, vague and lacking in confidence while talking to a sympathetic psychologist has some of these personality traits in other settings as well.

The child: his attitudes, behaviour and point of view

Observation of the child(ren) during the family interview can reveal important information about the referred child, and about the family. Is the referred child always a victim, perhaps, and required to give in to his siblings? Or does he tend to dominate? Do the children play creatively and together? Or does each child seem relatively isolated? Do they quarrel? Do they make a mess? Do they tidy up afterwards? Each observation is important as part of the diagnostic whole.

The psychologist should always encourage the child to answer for himself when asked a question. Sometimes it is difficult to prevent parents from answering for the child – indeed, it is not uncommon to find that parents assume that their children think and feel the way that *they* think and feel, and it may come as a surprise to them to hear their child say that he likes school, for example, when they had convinced themselves that he did not. The child may, perhaps, have complained from time to time about certain features in school life, and the parents have exaggerated his fears with their own anxieties. The psychologist needs to be able to step in tactfully if the child says something which appears to upset the parents: in this case, the focus of attention can sometimes usefully be shifted to the parents. For example, if the child says he likes school when the parents say he doesn't (because he has told them of a particular incident), the psychologist can ask the parents how *they* liked school. Perhaps they, too, had mixed feelings about it when they were young?

It is helpful if a child who is behaviourally disturbed can be encouraged to discuss what actually happens in school when he gets into trouble. He may complain that he is being bullied, or picked on; and may not be able to admit to being the aggressor. The psychologist acknowledges that he probably feels bullied or picked on at times – and then encourages him to talk about his *own* difficult behaviour. For example, it is possible to make it safe for the child to admit to being aggressive by saying, casually, that it is hard to do what is expected of one, or to keep one's temper. This allows the child to recognize that it is possible to talk about these difficulties. In other words, the child sees that the psychologist can accept his angry feelings and the difficult, stressful situation, though will not, of course, condone the aggressive act. A sympathetic understanding goes hand in hand with the recognition that people must learn to control themselves.

Listening to the child and to his parents, the psychologist can usefully try to imagine how life must be in that particular family for the referred child. Which of the parental personality characteristics would be liked, and which would be hard to live with? How would she try to adapt to the different parental personality characteristics while at the same time preserving a realistic and acceptable self-image? Would it be easy to understand exactly what was expected?

The psychologist–parent relationship

Meeting with parents for the first time, the psychologist will be forming her own subjective impressions of them and they of her. This has little to do with the nature of the communications which pass between them, and much to do with what might best be described as 'gut feelings'. One might feel very warmly towards some parents, and negatively towards others. Equally, it is possible to find oneself feeling a particularly strong sympathy for, or perhaps a dislike of, one or other of the spouses. (The psychologist can never be quite sure how the *parents* feel about *her*.) The natural tendency is to assume that these feelings reflect actual attributes in the parents, rather than some happy, or unhappy, interaction (or chemistry) between the parents' personalities and that of the psychologist. Earlier, during the discussion of object-relations theory, it was suggested that peoples' experience of their parents tends to colour the way in which they experience and react to other people later in their lives. In one sense, then, the psychologist reacts to the parents of the referred child as if they were her parents, and vice versa.

This is, of course, an over-simplification. Nevertheless, some degree of *transference* and *counter-transference* almost invariably takes place (Skynner, 1976a; Minuchin and Fishman, 1981). This is not used in the same way as analysts use it (i.e. by interpreting the person's reaction to the therapist in terms of his relationship with his own parents), although it needs to be taken into account. Thus, the psychologist may need to guard against the possibility of parents becoming too attached to or dependent on her. More important still is the need for the psychologist to consider the effects of counter-transference, that is, those often unreasonable feelings which one or more members of the family may arouse in her. Ideally, the psychologist who works regularly with families needs the opportunity to discuss these feelings with an experienced colleague. Although they may at times get in the way of helping a referred child, they can also be a valuable source of information for the psychologist. They can, for example, give the psychologist a clue about how individuals in a family may be affecting each other.

As a general rule, it may well be unhelpful to continue to work with parents who arouse very strong feelings in one, especially if these are negative. A colleague may find them less difficult, or it may be possible to meet only once and to make some other arrangements for helping the child. (One cannot, in any case, work regularly with all parents of referred children. Some degree of selection must be made, though it is important not to choose those parents who make one feel particularly good, since too friendly a relationship may not be helpful either!)

Most family therapists stress the need to keep a little distance between oneself and the family. Without this distance, one can miss seeing important interactions between family members, become drawn into the family system, or even into collusion with one member of the family. Keeping a distance, and allowing interactions to take place in front of one while gathering information little by little, it becomes possible to understand and to help *all* members of the family.

The psychologist's goals

During the initial interview, the psychologist has several goals in mind:

– to create a feeling of trust and confidence in the parents as

a foundation for possible future work with the family
- to try to gather as much factual information as possible without pressing the family too much
- to try to understand the family as a group or system, and the child as part of that system.

Sometimes these tasks are relatively easy and can be accomplished during one meeting; at other times they are more difficult and it is necessary to meet with the family several times. Sometimes it is virtually impossible, for many and complex reasons.

It is not always easy to develop a good (but not overinvolved) relationship with the child's parents, or to know in advance which aspects of life will be difficult or painful for the family to discuss. People vary greatly in their ability and willingness to talk about themselves and the past events in their lives. Some are surprisingly frank and open, and seem to enjoy talking about themselves; others are more reticent. Most people can, however, be encouraged to make some kind of communication with the psychologist, particularly if they are given the impression that their viewpoint is entirely acceptable to the psychologist, even if it is not agreed with.

As far as understanding the child's behaviour and general development in terms of his experience in his family system is concerned, this too is easier with some than with others. The psychologist's ability to do so increases as she develops her skills with working with families. Little by little, it becomes possible in many cases to move away from the idea of the child as 'possessing' a certain set of characteristics and towards the notion that his school behaviour, and his general performance, may reflect or represent certain attitudes, communications or experiences within the family.

9

Understanding and helping the child and his family

In Chapter 8 the initial process of meeting the child and his family was described. Attention must now be paid to the ways in which the psychologist can continue to involve the parents and to make use of their co-operation in an attempt to understand and help the child. They have important information which the psychologist needs; *she* has the ability to use that knowledge in a positive way for the benefit of all concerned.

Occasionally, the psychologist is able to understand or diagnose the reason for the child's difficulties quickly, and to know how her intervention should proceed. However, it is more often a question of a gradually increasing range and depth of understanding, with the psychologist testing certain hypotheses which she has in mind. If a particular theme seems promising, it is elaborated; if not, it is abandoned in favour of another. Psychologists with a knowledge of family therapy will be well aware that there are many different ways of describing and understanding family processes, and many different ways of using that understanding for the benefit of families, or of individuals. The choice of method depends very much on the individual worker, and is developed over a period of time, as she gains experience and confidence.

It is suggested, however, that certain models and methods of working with families are more useful in the practice of educational psychology than others, for reasons connected with the nature of the child's problem and the way in which the referral is perceived by the child's parents. This has already been mentioned in preceding chapters. From a practical point of view, it must always be remembered that the parents usually meet the psychologist because the child is perceived as having a problem at *school*. Although it will frequently be found that this is only one part of the story, it is always unhelpful and unwise to depart from this point of reference too rapidly. In my experience, parents often welcome the opportunity to talk about and explore their own attitudes and anxieties and to give the psychologist valuable information about wider worries (e.g. past events in the child's life, his present behaviour at home) if given time to develop confidence in the psychologist. They cannot be rushed, however much the psychologist is aware of the need to obtain certain information from them.

The most useful models for *general* application in the practice of educational psychology are those which give ample space for the expression of individual thought, feeling and opinions, and attention to important events (past and present) in the whole family's life-experience. Most family therapists stress the need for individuals to be heard in their own right, and for the airing of certain topics that have not previously been discussed, although they describe this in different ways and with different emphases. Working with children, I find Haldane and McCluskey's comments useful. They suggest that 'families tend to be trapped in repetitive patterns of behaviour and relationships which maintain the *status quo* and inhibit development, maturation and individuation', and that 'individuals in the family may find it impossible to cry out and be heard except in ways which are experienced by them and others as potentially destructive' (Haldane and McCluskey, 1982). Although this might seem to be rather too strongly expressed in the case of many of the children referred to the educational psychologist, the principles of free and open communication (including some limited 'crying out') still apply. These writers also suggest that such an expression of thought and feeling in the family session is itself helpful or therapeutic, even if the therapist/psychologist makes no intervention; though it is important for the psychologist to be able to facilitate and clarify the communications and to 'hold' the session should strong feelings be expressed.

Dare and Pincus (1978) discuss the need to bring into the open certain 'family secrets' which may not previously have been aired, though they are probably known to all or most members of the family. Minuchin and Fishman (1981) describe the way certain family 'myths' can be expelled as family members begin to communicate more openly with each other. Children, particularly, can benefit from being freed from certain fantasies about the past: the perceived need, for example, to measure up to the standards of an (imagined) perfect grandparent. The importance of recognizing that past events may be affecting present behaviour in certain members of the family is accepted by most family therapists. (See Bentovim and Kinston, 1978, for a description of the way in which present thoughts, feelings and actions of family members can be related to past events.) Parents may have certain unresolved conflicts from the past, connected with an unsatisfactory relationship with *their* parents. Thus, unexpressed feelings which belong to the grandparents may be projected by the parents on to the children unconsciously (see Lieberman, 1980).

The psychologist, therefore, recognizes the need to encourage free communication from family members. She knows that this will be a valuable exercise in its own right, and that it may also throw some light on possible reasons for the child's difficulties. She starts, then, by inviting them to contribute to a general discussion of the problem as they see it, and moves gradually towards broadening the subject and directing it in whatever way seems both relevant and profitable. In the process, she hopes to focus, whenever it seems appropriate, on topics which might have a bearing on the child's predicament, whatever that might be. Ideally, it should be possible to move between past and present, making links whenever appropriate and helpful, strengthening and encouraging certain attitudes and allaying certain fears and anxieties.

The techniques on which this approach is based can be considered under separate headings: communication, focusing (on certain important topics), reinforcement (of certain attitudes), modelling, and systems change.

Communication

The importance of the individual

In Chapter 8 emphasis was placed on the need to encourage individual family members to speak for themselves, and to listen to each other. The value of this cannot be overstated. Family relationships and family attitudes tend to be defined (and constrained) by communications between family members which are not necessarily true (or only half-true) and which need modifying. It may be apparent that the whole family *expects* a child always to be in trouble; or that they have convinced themselves that he is unable to learn to read. Their network of communications is based on these assumptions, often for no very good reason. However, the communications create a situation where the child begins to believe in and act upon the parental assumptions.

It is therefore particularly valuable if the child can be encouraged to give his own view of the situation, and to express his feelings about himself, his work and his relationships with others. The viewpoint he gives to the psychologist may or may not be factually correct, but it focuses the child's attention on his own importance as an individual. The psychologist's manner suggests that his viewpoint is valuable, and the child is encouraged to develop this, rather than act out parental expectations. His strengths, his desire for competence, his ability to overcome his weaknesses are taken for granted by the psychologist and communicated in a positive way to the child. Taking this approach, the psychologist occasionally runs into the problem that the child's viewpoint contradicts the parents'. Although it is extremely valuable for parents to hear the child addressed as though he were a competent person, able to answer for himself, it can be difficult if the child's attitudes differ from those attributed to him by the parent. The psychologist therefore needs to be able to balance the child's communications with a communication of her own designed to soften the blow, from the parents' point of view. In a very real sense, the psychologist often acts an interpreter between parent and child, and a facilitator of communication between them.

It is also important for the psychologist to recognize that each individual's viewpoint must be respected as important and valid to *them*, even if it occasionally arouses both anger and anxiety in the listener (i.e. the psychologist). Minuchin gives a good example of this, when he describes talking to a young mother who had been acting violently towards her young child. The mother complained bitterly that the child had spoilt their Christmas Day, a viewpoint which Minuchin took seriously, offering sympathy to the mother before attempting to move towards any change in the parental attitudes. (Minuchin and Fishman, 1981.)

Clarifying certain communications

During the course of a family session it can quite often be observed that children are genuinely confused by their parents' attitudes and communications, and are in fact unaware of what their parents really want or expect of them. Parents may be so incensed by a school teacher that they fail to see that the child's actions have been reprehensible, and so fail to tell him that they are annoyed. Or perhaps they may be so convinced that their child is different in a special way (dyslexic, gifted, handicapped) that they ignore the need to give sensible instructions to the child; for example, that he needs to try hard, conform to the rules other children conform to, etc.

The opportunity is always taken to clarify the parental viewpoint in the child's hearing. Have the mother and father told the child that they want him to behave and try hard? That he must do his homework – even if the next-door child does not? Are the parents speaking with one voice? Or does there appear to be collusion between one parent and the child? On the other hand, have the parents listened to the child? Do they know he sometimes feels lonely, upset, unhappy, angry?

Occasionally, one is aware of communications that are not merely confusing, but are strikingly deviant, or a double-bind. There is unfortunately some disagreement between therapists on the nature of (or even the existence of) double-bind and deviant communications between parents and children. Although at one time much emphasis was placed on the importance of certain types of parental communication in 'driving their offspring mad', it has recently received much less attention. In my view, this is a pity. Working regularly with young children and their families, it is quite common to hear messages from parent to child (or from parent to the psychologist *about* the child) which place a child in an untenable no-win situation. Two examples of this type of communication are given below.

(1) *Psychologist* (of a very immature little girl who had recently begun to develop confidence in herself): 'Anna seems to be growing up and taking more responsibility for herself now.'

Mother (with a smile): 'Yes. She's getting a big girl now. She's getting quite cheeky. Anna knows she mustn't be cheeky to her mother ...'

(2) *Psychologist* (discussing where a 10-year-old boy does his homework): 'How do you manage – does Stephen have his own bedroom?'

Mother 'Yes, but he shares with his sister. He gets very nervous at night and she keeps him company.'

Stephen 'I don't like sharing with her.'

Mother 'He gets *very* nervous ...'

It is not of course possible to say how a child interprets such comments. Is Anna left with the feeling that growing up is a positive, or a negative attribute in herself? Is the 10-year-old boy *really* nervous, or does he need to share with his sister for some other reason? Many adults have a confusing way of talking, and their children have to develop techniques for coping with this. On the other hand, it is not unreasonable to suppose that some children are left with feelings of despair, confusion, anger or guilt if continually subjected to this type of communication. Such feelings must inevitably affect their attitudes to other adults, including their teachers.

In these, and similar, situations the psychologist can usefully act as interpreter between parent and child. In the first case, for example, it can be stated that growing up (for a child) means *both* being more responsible *and* at times, more 'naughty'. It would be very surprising if Anna were *not* naughty occasionally. Perhaps they could talk about it in more detail? In the second case, the psychologist can tactfully explore whether Stephen really feels nervous, and if there is the possibility for him to have his own room. If not, he must be helped to come to terms with this, rather than be told that he needs to share because he is nervous.

Non-verbal communications

It is not uncommon to find, when meeting the family, that parental comments sometimes contradict their facial expression. Parents may tell the child that he is naughty or lazy, but with a smile on their face. One cannot be sure about how the child experiences this paradoxical situation, but it is worth asking him whether he realizes that Mummy (or Daddy) is cross. His reply may be uncertain, and the psychologist need not press the point; but she can use it as a foundation for exploring other attitudes in the family: do people always understand each other? is it possible to say what you really think, mean or feel? do people listen if you do?

Non-verbal communications and the behaviour of the child(ren) during the family sessions are often very important too. This was mentioned in Chapter 8 as part of the initial diagnostic session, but the psychologist should continue to be aware of the implications of the ways in which the child behaves during the sessions. Does he fidget and twitch when the parent talks? Perhaps he can be encouraged to speak for himself more freely, and the parent encouraged to listen. Does he constantly ('accidentally') spill sand? Maybe it is necessary to talk about the child's play at home, and whether the parent might perhaps worry unduly about tidiness and cleanliness. Does he continually deny his younger brother access to toys? Perhaps the psychologist should discuss the natural rivalry that exists between children, and the way the parents cope with it.

Focusing on certain important topics

The psychologist recognizes that certain important events in the family's life-experience may have had a profound effect on the child, even if others are unaware of this. She also recognizes that certain topics have almost certainly been insufficiently aired or discussed, so that the child may have misconceptions about them. Perhaps the simplest example of this is in the case of a divorce, when the child is left with the feeling that one parent or another was at fault – or even that he himself was at fault. Anger, uncertainty, confusion and conflicting loyalties can all combine to produce conflict in the child with resulting behavioural disturbance, or lack of progress at school.

Topics which the psychologist feels should be aired will not necessarily easily be brought into the conversation. Parents can be invited to contribute ideas of their own as to certain factors which might have upset the child and inhibited his progress.

Some parents seize this opportunity with enthusiasm, and are able to recognize that, for example, a divorce or a long-term illness might have made difficulties for the child. This allows the psychologist to move towards some understanding of the relationship between the past event and present behaviour and performance in the child. Other parents seem unable to talk about themselves, or about past events.

Dare and Pincus (1978) speak of family secrets – secrets which are nearly always known to family members, but which seem too painful to discuss. Such secrets are often concerned with past events in the parents' lives which have made an impact, and are associated with a good deal of suffering. Two examples of such experiences are given below.

Lucy, aged 5½, was referred when her infant school teachers found her behaviour puzzling. She was confused in the classroom, totally lacking in concentration, almost completely silent. However, on occasions she could produce very good work very quickly, so that they knew she was not retarded. The headteacher knew the parents, and knew that the mother had been depressed for many years following the death of a baby born before Lucy. The parents agreed to the referral to the psychologist, but said they did not want to discuss the baby in front of Lucy. This was agreed to by the psychologist.

Interestingly, and fortunately, the parents themselves brought up the topic after a while in Lucy's presence, giving the psychologist the opportunity to discuss the death with the parents and to share their feelings of guilt and loss. Lucy listened to the conversation and occasionally asked questions. The intervention appeared to help her, and she began to settle down in school.

In another 'family secrets' case, the situation was less satisfactory. *Martin*, aged 13, was referred for an almost total lack of progress at school. During the individual session he drew a hearse and surrounded his drawing with black. Although the nature of the drawing was not revealed to the parents, since it was done during an individual session, the parents were encouraged to talk about themselves and other members of the family. They revealed that another child had died, about five years previously. It seemed that Martin's academic progress stopped at that point. Unfortunately, the parents did not wish to discuss the topic which was, for them, finished – although this would probably have been helpful to Martin. Reluctantly, the psychologist had to break contact with the parents and help Martin in other ways.

In other, less painful, circumstances it is still valuable if the parents can look back to experiences in their own lives which might have a bearing on the child's problems. Two brief examples are given.

John was referred when underachieving at school. It was apparent that his father had never managed to come to terms with his own academic failure at 11+ as a boy, and was putting far too much pressure on John, who was becoming increasingly resistant to the idea of school work. The psychologist sympathized with the father, and recognized that this failure would have made him very anxious for John to succeed. Eventually, he was able to admit that perhaps he *had* put too much pressure on the boy.

Tracy was referred in infant school as generally 'difficult' – she was confused and attention-seeking. Her mother found her 'impossible' at home. Encouraged to talk about her relationship with her own mother, Tracy's mother said: 'Maybe I can't get on with Tracy because of the way I felt about *my* mother.' This self-insight gave the psychologist the opportunity to encourage the mother to explore further her own attitudes, experiences and behaviour with benefit to the child.

During the process of sharing certain past experiences, the psychologist needs to be able to step in if certain communications appear too painful for some to bear. In one family session with a mother and her daughter, the girl, who had been excluded from school for disruptive behaviour, moved away from the subject of school and attacked her mother for excessive and solitary drinking at home. The mother looked shocked and hurt. The psychologist was able to step in and interpret the girl's comments as concern for her mother's welfare rather than criticism, which led to a positive discussion of the problems which the mother and daughter had faced together since the father had left home – problems which had contributed significantly to the girl's behavioural disturbance. This *positive connotation* of a person's apparently negative behaviour can be used in many different ways. It may be part of a *redefinition* of the problems, which can lead the therapist to making a *paradoxical intervention* (see Minuchin and Fishman, 1981).

Reinforcing certain (appropriate) parental attitudes

There is, inevitably, scope for differences of opinion on what constitutes appropriate parenting. Equally, there is scope for disagreement on what is, or is not, unacceptable child behaviour. Anyone who undertakes to work with families is aware of the need to be as objective and as reasonable as possible about this, and to try not to let personal experience and prejudice cloud the issues.

The psychologist can ask herself certain questions about parental attitudes, while bearing in mind the need for some flexibility on the subject:

- do the parents appear to have realistic expectations of the child, with regard to his age and ability?
- do they seem able to set sensible limits on his behaviour, and to agree between themselves on these limits?
- do they seem able to tolerate the ordinary variability of the child's behaviour (e.g. occasional sulks, untidy bedrooms etc.)?

It can occasionally be seen that parental attitudes and expectations are entirely inappropriate to the child's age and needs.

A 10-year-old boy, referred for stealing at school, had been taking responsibility for himself for a number of years: taking himself on public transport, shopping for his mother and for his own clothes, etc. He had managed to keep himself going until the parents separated. His stealing alerted the school (and the psychologist) to the need for intervention.

A 14-year-old girl was constantly in trouble for not doing her homework. On investigation it was found that she and her parents had a battle each evening about the homework. Further investigation revealed that she was allowed out late to visit public houses with older boys. The parents who were so involved (over-involved) with her homework appeared unwilling, or unable, to take steps to prevent her visiting public houses and to get her to bed at a reasonable time.

These are examples of what most people would probably consider inappropriate parenting. In both cases the children were in trouble at school, though the ways in which they behaved reflected unsatisfactory and confused parental attitudes at home. It would, however, have been unhelpful for the psychologist to criticize the parents' attitudes directly. These attitudes represent 'reality' for the parents, based on their *own* view of what is or is not appropriate. A more circumspect approach is needed if the child is to be helped. For example, in the first case the boy was praised for his grown-up efforts to look after himself, and the mother sympathized with for her own domestic difficulties. The psychologist then suggested that maybe the stealing was a sign that everything was too much for *both* of them. In the second case, the parents were commended for their desire to encourage the girl to do her homework, but perhaps she was now old enough to think about this herself? How did they feel about her visiting public houses? Maybe if she weren't out quite so late ...?

In both cases, the psychologist assumed that all parties really want to do the right thing, but can't quite manage it. Both parties are praised for their efforts and a positive connotation put on their behaviour wherever possible before any move is made to suggest possible change.

An important technique when working with families is that of stressing the normality of certain behaviour: it is normal for children to say that they dislike certain aspects of school; normal for adolescents to be rude, moody, short-tempered, lazy; normal for siblings to fight with each other, envy each other, want individual attention. Equally, it is normal for parents to feel depressed, irritable, despairing with themselves, each other and their children from time to time. It helps to talk about it. Anxiety levels are lowered; people feel better and more confident; matters tend to improve.

Modelling

This technique is particularly useful in families with young children. It can be used by the psychologist as a matter of course, even if there is nothing 'wrong' with parental attitudes, but is, of course, particularly useful with those families where parents are immature and lacking in self-confidence.

Where parents have difficulty with their young children it is quite often either because they are (a) uncertain about what to allow or to permit, so that their uncertainty is communicated to the child; (b) very inconsistent (spoiling the child one minute, punishing him the next); or (c) too rigid and inflexible. The psychologist during the family session(s) quite often has the opportunity to demonstrate to the parents that 2-year-old children can be *lifted* down from a desk/away from a wastepaper basket, rather than shouted at; that older children can be gently but firmly suppressed if they make too much noise; that spilt sand and toys on the floor are unimportant; that it is important to *listen* to children as well as to talk to them.

The psychologist can make use of a child's untidiness in many ways, according to the apparent needs of the child and the family. With a family which is obviously very burdened she can tell the parents – or perhaps more often the single mother – that she will clear up the mess since the parent 'has enough to do at home'. On the other hand, she can let a grateful parent help her to tidy up if it seems important to the parent. She can often use untidiness in her room as an introduction to the topic of the children's behaviour at home – and then to the domestic situation more generally.

Changing the system

People who work with families, basing their intervention on family-systems theory, usually assume there is an unsatisfactory system in operation which one needs to recognize and change. There are however different ways of defining and describing these 'unsatisfactory' systems, as well as different ways of intervening for the benefit of the person who appears to be at a disadvantage in the system: some therapists emphasize the importance of past events; others concentrate on family transactions which can be observed in the 'here and now'. Although the topic is too complex for a full discussion here, certain points are particularly relevant to the educational psychologist.

It is suggested that the educational psychologist may not become aware of an unsatisfactory system (in the pure A → B → C → A sense of the term) when faced with the family of a referred child. She is, in my experience, much more likely to be faced with a situation where there is stress or anxiety as described in preceding chapters, or where communications are tending to 'trap' the child (inadvertently) in an unsatisfactory role, or to produce a situation of confusion for him.

Occasionally, however, parents tell the psychologist how they handle their children in such a way that it is apparent that there is an unsatisfactory system in operation. A parent might, for example, tell the psychologist that the child is always late for school because, no matter how often she calls him, he cannot get out of bed in the morning. The psychologist might then comment that there is a relationship between the calling and the staying in bed: 'The more you call, the more he clings to his bed, perhaps.' It is often admitted that this is so, and the psychologist can go on to suggest to the child that getting up is his own responsibility, so softening the blow by recognizing that it is quite difficult to do this. Does he have his own alarm clock? He sounds like a competent person in many ways, maybe he could listen for his alarm, and get up when it rings?

The psychologist might also ask the parents to discuss between themselves methods of helping the child. Listening to their discussion, it may become apparent that there are differing viewpoints and that one parent is colluding with the child against the other. Some parents can see this once it is pointed out to them; others, more fragile and anxious, may need time and help to work towards this understanding.

10

Troubled children, troubled family systems: two case-histories

In Chapter 9 it was suggested that an understanding of the processes that both create and maintain the system in a particular family has wide application, even when it is a question of helping children who do not appear to live in troubled families. It is, nevertheless, unfortunately the case that many referred children *do* live in families which are in one way or another 'troubled'. It therefore seems appropriate to describe in some detail the help offered to two such children before moving on to discuss the wider application of family-systems theory.

First, it is important to outline briefly what is meant by a 'troubled' family system. Although there are many different ways of approaching the subject, it seems reasonable to suggest that a troubled family system is one where either past events or present attitudes (or both) are contributing to a state of affairs which tends to produce behavioural disturbance and/or lack of developmental progress in a child or children of the family. This is not to suggest that the parents are in any way morally at fault, or unwilling to do the best for their children. Frequently, they are themselves victims of past events in their own lives, which makes it difficult for them to meet their own children's needs. They do their best by their own lights, though the children are not actually receiving what *they* need for their developmental growth.

The two children described in this chapter lived in family systems which could be described as troubled. *Angela*, aged 5½, was referred for hyperactive attention-seeking behaviour at school. A meeting with her parents and a discussion of past events indicated that Angela's behaviour was related to unsatisfactory experiences in her past life, and to somewhat unsatisfactory adult attitudes in the present. *Susie*, aged 12, was referred in the second term of secondary school, for lie-telling, devious behaviour and poor relationships with other children. Parental attitudes were well-meaning but very rigid and somewhat punitive.

In both these cases, it would have been possible to help the children within the school. However, the psychologist was immediately aware of the relationship between the family system and the child's behaviour in both cases *and* (even more important) the parents were obviously ready to co-operate, so that family sessions were quickly started. Intervention in the school proved unnecessary in both cases.

Angela

Angela was referred for attention-seeking, hyperactive behaviour at school, poor relationships with other children, and an inability to accept even very simple discipline.

The parents (her father and stepmother) brought her for interview and assessment. Father was thin and anxious-looking, stepmother rather large and friendly. They expressed concern about the referral and asked almost immediately if it meant that the child was backward. Since the reports on Angela's school work were quite good, they could be reassured immediately about this.

Angela sat on the father's lap and was very silent during the initial part of the interview. The psychologist said that it was felt by school staff that although Angela could work quite well she sometimes seemed not to have her mind on her work, and also found it difficult to do what was expected of her. It would help if they could get together to find out why, in the hope that this might help Angela settle down. The psychologist also suggested that it was always a good idea to look at this kind of problem while the child was young, rather than waiting for the difficulties to build up over a period of time.

Angela's parents proved quite ready to talk about themselves, and to refer to the considerable number of difficult life-events which Angela had experienced. Angela's mother had left with another man when Angela was a baby, and the father had struggled alone to bring her up while continuing to work. Angela had had to contend with temporary fostering, and a long period of time at a day nursery. She also had the difficulty of occasional, disruptive visits to her mother. More recently, she had had to get to know her stepmother, and to adapt to sharing her father with her new mother.

From the parents' point of view, things were going quite well. They were making a new life together successfully. They were, however, under constant pressure from Angela's mother, and were worried that Angela's behaviour tended to deteriorate after she had been to visit her for a weekend. They claimed that Angela's natural mother tended to spoil her.

From Angela's point of view, there were several difficulties. These might be summarized as follows:

- the need to come to terms with the knowledge that her natural mother (even though she now spoiled her) had in fact abandoned her
- difficulties associated with being handled by many different adults (e.g. foster parents, nurses at the day nursery, etc.)
- the problem of sharing her father with a new stepmother
- the problem of accepting discipline from her stepmother
- the difficulty of avoiding the temptation to play off one (spoiling) mother against another (disciplining) mother.

In addition to these difficulties, Angela was probably also adversely affected by the personalities of the adults in her life. Her father had been very young when married for the first time.

He had suffered from depression during adolescence and his first marriage had been very stormy. The mother (unseen) was also apparently very immature. The stepmother, though kind to Angela, was at times a little off-hand and bossy. In short, Angela's unhappy early experience had made her very vulnerable and, though the father and the stepmother were trying to make a successful trio, they were not really giving Angela the extra support and understanding she needed as the result of her early difficulties. They tended to be rather repressive and over-disciplining, demanding unrealistically high standards of behaviour. The psychologist also felt, though this was not admitted directly, that the stepmother, though kind to Angela, was a little resentful of her presence.

Individual assessment Alone with Angela, the psychologist suggested she drew. After some discussion, Angela drew herself 'at the seaside' – a rather pathetic-looking drawing of an armless figure, without nose and mouth. It contrasted sharply with Angela's obvious competence in other areas – counting, sharing, reading, etc. Although it is not necessary to make accurate, diagnostic observations from the drawing, there was undoubtedly the feeling conveyed of a helpless immature infant 'all at sea'.

Angela was encouraged to play with the dolls' house, and to talk about herself. Again, the contrast between the 'competent' Angela and the lost infant was apparent. Angela's conversation was confused, unfocused, and difficult to follow. Her play was also purposeless and disorganized. Only when actually 'made' to do something (e.g. count) did she do it, and then only for a short period of time. Indeed, it was generally noticeable that Angela functioned when 'made' to do something, but was lost and uncreative when left to her own devices. (A formal intelligence test was not undertaken. Angela was only 5½, could count well and share; had a reading age of 6.03 and could write her name and a few simple words. She was obviously of at least average intelligence. Since her concentration was so poor, a formal test would not have done her justice, nor was it really necessary.)

At the end of the individual session, the parents were invited back in. The psychologist spoke about Angela's obvious intelligence, and about how she was not actually able to make the most of it because things had been worrying her. No blame or criticism was implied, but the psychologist suggested it would be useful if they could meet again and talk about the different things that had happened to Angela in her life, and how to help her come to terms with them.

During the subsequent sessions, it became apparent that Angela, who had at first been a rather deprived and confused child in her original family system, was in danger of becoming a 'pawn' in a complex system of three adults: mother, stepmother and father. Her natural mother was tending to spoil and indulge her during her visits. Her stepmother, on the other hand, was tending to over-react to this by being more than usually strict. The father seemed to be showing signs of being torn between the two women. Though resentful of his first wife's attitude, he was also (somewhat reluctantly) a little critical of his second wife. Occasionally he found himself drawn in to support his second wife against Angela in situations where his natural instinct was to be more lenient. These stresses and strains were gradually revealed over the three to four months during which the psychologist and the family met together (five sessions of approximately three-quarters of an hour each in all). The work focused on the following points.

(1) Practical arrangements: visiting mother; fetching and carrying.
(2) Discipline. Who makes the rules? Do the father and stepmother agree with each other and support each other? Can they accept that *their* rules are almost bound to be different from the attitudes of Angela's natural mother?

(3) Angela's point of view: a discussion of past events and how they had affected her. A recognition that her two mothers were different people with different standards and ideas, and that she could learn to come to terms with this.
(4) The need for Angela's father and stepmother to have time for themselves – perhaps taking advantage of Angela's weekends with her natural mother for outings on their own.
(5) A suggestion to the parents that the three adults get together to discuss arrangements, discipline, etc. between them.

It is interesting to note that although Angela appeared to benefit from the family sessions, this last recommendation, which might seem the most obvious, was never properly carried out. The three adults did not appear to change very much during the course of the psychologist's intervention. Angela's change and improvement could be attributed to a coming to terms with the reality of her life, and perhaps to the recognition of what had gone before was not her responsibility, and could be safely left behind and outgrown.

Susie

Susie was referred after one term at secondary school because she stole another child's purse. Prior to this event her behaviour had often given the teachers cause for concern (constant lie-telling, devious behaviour, provocative behaviour towards other children, poor performance in academic work).

The school had had occasion to get in touch with the parents several times over different incidents during Susie's first term. After a while, however, teachers had become aware that this was counter-productive. The parents had become very angry with the school, and staff also had the impression that Susie was being too rigorously disciplined at home as the result of their contact with the parents. At the time of referral, staff were aware that Susie was a seriously disturbed, confused and unhappy little girl, and their annoyance with her had largely changed to bewilderment and concern.

The parents were invited by the psychologist to an initial interview to discuss 'one or two difficulties which Susie has been having at school'. They seemed quite willing to attend. At the family interview, the parents were seen to be rather older than the psychologist had expected. There were also two other daughters, Kate, aged 10, and Faye, 4. All three girls were neatly dressed and absolutely silent.

Susie was taken for an individual session early in the proceedings in the hope that she would be more communicative alone. This proved not to be so. She was reluctant to say anything, giving the impression that it might be dangerous to answer questions truthfully, even if they were simple and straightforward. The Wechsler Intelligence Test (WISC) was started, but discontinued when Susie showed great anxiety. She drew a house – reluctantly – when it was suggested she might draw. The drawing was equivalent to one that might have been done by a 7-year-old. Yet Susie did not seem unintelligent. The few responses she gave to the WISC were sensible and mature. Her unresponsiveness, relatively unusual in any child during individual assessment, suggested to the psychologist that Susie had quite a serious problem, which might well reflect difficulties within the family.

When the family were all together again they seemed more relaxed, but it was obvious that the father was exercising considerable control over the girls. They all showed a great reluctance to answer for themselves, and looked to him to answer for them, which he almost invariably did.

The family members could be described as follows.

Father. A large, bland man with a manner which was rather placating. He often spoke for the whole family, describing the things they did in terms of what *he* wanted them to do. If, for example, the children were asked what games they liked playing, or what television programmes they liked to watch, father stepped in with comments on what he thought they should play or watch. He gave the impression of a man who wanted to impress the psychologist by his reasonableness, and his ability to father his children.

Mother. A very tense and angry woman. While father's manner was smooth and placating, hers was blaming and attacking. If one member of the family said something she disagreed with, she leapt in immediately to contradict. At times, she would be jocular and teasing. Later, she told the psychologist she had been in care as in child, and brought up in a children's home. This had obviously been an unhappy experience for her which had left its mark on her personality.

The parents had married when they were both over 30. Though the mother had been independent for a number of years (indeed, was forced to be independent), the father had lived at home with his own mother prior to marriage.

Susie. A tense, confused child. Later, she began to reveal some strengths which were not initially apparent. She had, for example, a good sense of humour, and an ability to express herself clearly and thoughtfully when relaxed and more confident.

Kate. A very controlled little girl. She was less often in trouble with her parents than Susie. In many ways, the 'good one' of the family.

Faye. An immature little girl, with some speech difficulties.

It seemed as though this might be a difficult family to work with. The mother was very touchy and sensitive, responding with a few short, sharp words. Father did all the talking. The girls were completely silent, and very serious-looking. They made one feel uncomfortable, partly because of the suspicion that the father's method of disciplining the girls might be harsh. Beneath the bland exterior, there was almost certainly a man of iron. However, Susie was very much in need of help. Her behaviour suggested a child who could not continue much longer without either bursting out or breaking down. Even if this did not happen, it seemed unlikely that she could continue to attend her present school since her behaviour made for serious difficulties in the classroom. The family was therefore offered another appointment and, rather to the psychologist's surprise, it was accepted without question. Indeed, they became enthusiastic and regular attenders, never late for appointments, and never missing any. Six sessions of about three-quarters of an hour each were held in all, at two- to three-week intervals. Two follow-up appointments were offered.

The family system It was felt that father was too powerful in the family system, not only in a negative and obvious sense, but in exercising an excessive and overpowering control over the girls at an emotional level. The mother was functioning rather like an older sister (or perhaps a brother, since her manner was rather boyish). Her behaviour was quite destructive of the children, yet at times she could be friendly and good-humoured. The hierarchy of the family might have been indicated thus:

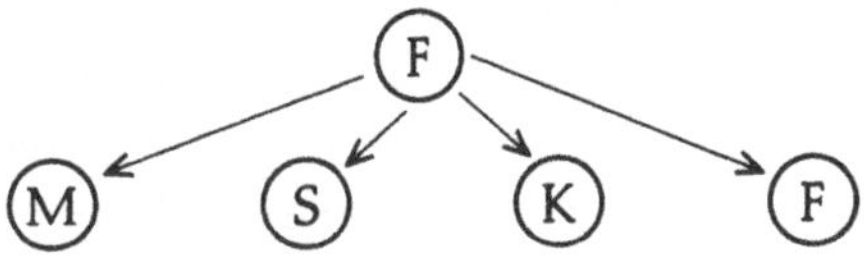

with father taking on the role of both mother and father to four 'children'.

It was apparent to the psychologist that the father's need to resort to excessive control had been learnt from his own parents – particularly his mother, who had been very punitive. It also appeared that the children's mother had suffered quite considerably from her time in a children's home, and often had unrealistic expectations of the girls – Susie, particularly, was often expected to take on a parental role, bringing her mother cups of tea, offering to do the washing up, etc.

Yet the family was not without its strengths. Though controlling, rather punitive, and with standards and expectations that were somewhat unrealistic, the parents had managed to give the girls affection and care. In some ways, it could be said that the family system had been good during the early years of the children's lives, but was showing signs of strain now that Susie was growing older. There was a need for change and relaxation in the parental discipline. Susie needed to stretch her wings, and not to feel that she was impossible if she didn't bring her mother tea, or do the washing up on time.

The therapeutic approach The psychologist's first task was to establish the right of the children to speak for themselves. This right was not actually stated, but by continually addressing the children individually and by listening carefully to the reply – cutting out father if necessary – the psychologist established little by little their right to their own viewpoint. On the occasions when it was necessary to cut out father, the psychologist turned back to him when the conversation with the children was over, and asked *his* opinion, treating it as separate from the child's (and neither inferior nor superior to it).

The second part of the therapy was that of increasing the parents' self-esteem. The father's controlling manner and the mother's sudden outbursts were recognized as manifestations of immature personalities, which were damaging to the children. Nevertheless, it was obvious that the parents had done their best for the children, and that much of their behaviour had been both effective and caring. The psychologist commented on these positive aspects. At the same time, the parents were encouraged to discuss their more negative feelings related to past experiences. The topic of physical punishment provided a good opportunity for this. Susie mentioned, cautiously, that Dad hit her, and this allowed the psychologist to ask him if he had been hit as a child. Given this opportunity, the father was able to express resentment about his own mother's heavy methods of discipline.

He was also able to accept the psychologist's suggestion that this might have seemed to him the only way of bringing up children, but perhaps another method would be better.

The third component of the therapy was that of allowing some degree of licence in the psychologist's room. The children were encouraged to play during the sessions. On the whole Susie seemed to prefer to sit and talk, but Katie and Faye played, and enjoyed the opportunity to make something of a mess. The psychologist made light of the sand on the floor, and refused to let the parents clear it up. This approach to untidiness has a dual purpose with very formal parents. It allows them to see that spilt sand (mess) is a trivial matter. At the same time, it allows the psychologist to 'parent the parent' by refusing help in clearing it up. (It is, however, worth commenting to the parents, when allowing children to be untidy, that one recognizes that they cannot necessarily allow such freedom at home. This is said to avoid colluding with the children.)

As the therapy proceeded, the whole family relaxed and responded well. They proved all to have more sense of humour and intelligence than one might first have thought. The girls were allowed to speak for themselves, and the parents used the sessions to talk about the various difficulties associated with bringing up children.

In summary, the therapy consisted of:

- close attention to the individual needs of all family members (the need to be listened to, understood, respected)
- modelling of good, parenting behaviour (listening to the children, allowing a certain amount of mess on the floor)
- allowing the children to express the previously unexpressable ('Dad hits me')
- increasing parental self-esteem by listening without criticism even when the parents were unreasonable, and sympathizing when appropriate for past events.

Susie's improvement was noticeable after a few weeks. A year later, she was performing at the average level of her age group and had many good friends at school. The other children were also making satisfactory progress in school.

11

Partnership and the family system

In Chapter 4 certain partnership schemes were described, where parents were taught techniques by the psychologist to apply directly to their children. Such schemes included those where parents were taught behaviour modification skills to use with their physically or mentally handicapped or behaviourally disturbed children; and techniques such as paired-reading where parents read regularly in unison with their children. The doubts that were expressed about some of these schemes might be summarized as follows: it is inappropriate to think of co-opting the parents of a referred child into a partnership scheme unless one is able to take into consideration both stress factors within the family system and any possible relationship between the child's symptoms and the family system.

It is therefore suggested that partnership schemes, regardless of their nature, are likely to be more effective if the psychologist works with an understanding of family processes in general terms; and, if possible, with an understanding of the nature of the 'system' in the particular family with which she is concerned. At times, this seems essential. In those cases where a child's symptoms seem to be a direct reflection of certain unsatisfactory factors in the family system, it seems entirely inappropriate to involve the parents in a scheme which involves applying certain techniques to the child as though they were *outside* the system which is tending to produce or to maintain the child's symptoms.

It is, however, easier to see in some cases than others how the child's symptoms might be related to the family system. In a case described by Douglas (1981), a child's soiling seemed to be related to certain family factors – mainly a poor marital relationship. The parents were given instructions to follow to help their child stop soiling, but attention was also paid to the family system, in particular to the marital relationship. Can one make a comparison between this case, and cases where a child might be referred with reading difficulties? I would suggest that it is always useful to look at the family in general terms, and to try to assess the strengths and weaknesses of the family system before involving the parents in a partnership scheme.

The following two cases are examples of children who were helped directly by their parents who followed certain directions given to them by the psychologist. In each case, attention was also paid to certain family factors as part of the scheme to help the children.

Mary

Mary was referred at 7 years with a general lack of progress at school. Teachers felt that Mary was developmentally slightly retarded in a general sense, and there was some question as to whether she might need special education. However, her IQ was within the average range (verbal IQ 85 on WISC–R). The draw-a-man test (Goodenough) gave a score equivalent to that of a child of 6.06 years. She had just begun to read (5.09 on the Holborn scale).

Mary's parents were relatively unsophisticated people, who almost immediately expressed anxiety (rather obliquely) about the possibility that Mary might be mentally retarded. They were reassured immediately on that score. The psychologist was then told that the father had been at an ESN(M) school, and was still almost illiterate. There was another daughter, aged 5, who was much brighter than Mary.

It was felt that the family system was reasonably stable and harmonious, and that Mary's relationship with her mother was good. However, it was apparent that two factors were tending to make things a little difficult for Mary: first, the father's anxiety, which arose principally from his own feelings of inadequacy dating back to his childhood, was unhelpful; secondly, Mary's much brighter and livelier sister was threatening to outshine her.

Help was planned for Mary on the following lines.

(1) Mother and Mary were taught to use a paired-reading technique together, which they were to use at bedtime.
(2) Father was to keep her younger sister occupied while this was going on.
(3) The psychologist met with the family once a month to allow the parents to discuss their own anxieties about themselves and their children. This was particularly slanted towards the father, with the psychologist paying attention to the need to increase his self-esteem. During these sessions, efforts were also made to increase Mary's self-esteem, and feelings of competence.

This approach proved helpful, and Mary managed to make progress along with the slower members of her class.

David

David, aged 3.8 years, was referred after three weeks at nursery school. He had little language and seemed unable to understand even simple instructions. His behaviour towards other children was unpredictable, and sometimes aggressive. His motor control was poor. This information presented the psychologist with a pessimistic picture. However, by the time he was seen by the psychologist, about six weeks later, he had begun to settle down at school and to accept certain rules of behaviour. His speech remained immature, and relatively limited.

Individual assessment David was quite co-operative with the psychologist, though verbal communication was impossible in view of his severe speech difficulties. The Merrill–Palmer Test and parts of the McCarthy Scale of Children's Abilities were administered, with mixed results. Although he managed jigsaw-puzzle-type tests well, he was weak on tests involving manual control. In general terms he was functioning in the 'low-average' ability range.

Interview with parents An interview with the parents revealed information which was diagnostically important. They were a young, highly intelligent couple who had married when the wife became pregnant towards the end of her studies at university. The husband had been completing his studies and had been living away from home for much of David's early life. The wife had been seriously depressed following the child's birth, and for about a year David has been cared for by a series of childminders. There was no history of perinatal truauma and early milestones (sitting, crawling, walking) had been normal. He had been an 'easy baby', and had been left largely to his own devices in his cot or pram.

It seemed likely that David's early experience had been insufficiently stimulating for his developmental needs, and also that he must have felt confused and disoriented by the lack of stable adult figures. At the time when he was seen for psychological assessment the parents were reunited, the mother better able to cope with David, and the father in steady employment. It was suggested that they could help David in several ways: by talking and listening to him, by playing with him, and by introducing into everyday conversation certain topics and ideas – for example, naming cutlery, as the table was laid, counting biscuits on to the plate, talking about an activity (dressing, washing) as it was undertaken.

Nevertheless, it was clear that there were other, more personal, family factors that needed to be discussed: there was, for example, the problem of the father's job, which was relatively boring and with few prospects; the mother was resentful that she had had to cut short her own education when she became pregnant, and their relationship with each other was uncertain, with much unexpressed anger. Most important of all, perhaps, both parents felt considerable guilt at the thought that they had neglected David's needs during the formative years of his life. It was explained to them that it was likely that there were several, unknown, reasons why David's speech and motor ability were so poor, and that they should not blame themselves in any way.

Counselling and support for the parents were offered over a period of about a year. During this time David made reasonable progress in nursery school, with extra specialized help in speech therapy as well.

Deciding not to use a partnership scheme

Two cases have been briefly described, where the psychologist used the parents as partners in a scheme to help their own child, while at the same time paying attention to certain factors in the families which were related, directly or indirectly, to the child's symptoms. Here, it is suggested that occasionally the psychologist can profitably decide *not* to use a child's parent(s) in a partnership scheme at all on the basis of certain family factors, but find help for the child in other directions.

Matthew, aged 8, was referred with severe reading difficulties and poor general progress in school. His behaviour was restless, aggressive, moody. Indeed, he had presented difficulties in school for a number of years.

Matthew had an IQ of 108 and a reading age of 6.03. There was little of significance during the individual assessment session, though a session with both Matthew and his mother was very revealing. It appeared that they lived alone together and that before Matthew's father left he had been continually drunk and violent for a number of years. This had been hard enough for Matthew to bear, but his position now was only slightly improved. Matthew's mother was a very over-protective woman in her late 40s, in poor health and emotionally very dependent on Matthew.

It was felt that the mother should not be asked to help him to read, partly because she was burdened enough herself with poor health and partly because her relationship with Matthew was too close and too anxious. Help was offered from elsewhere – individual sessions with a teacher, who was also able to take on a counselling role, and therefore to help Matthew come to terms with some of the social and emotional difficulties which faced him.

Partnership with parents on a larger scale

Ten years ago, few schools allowed parents past their doors without an appointment. Today, it is increasingly common for parents to be closely involved with many school activities, particularly in infant schools. Parents are often encouraged to come into the classroom, and co-opted as helpers – hearing children read, helping with the dressing and undressing of younger children when necessary, accompanying teachers and children on school outings. Although not all schools encourage parental involvement, it seems likely that the trend will continue.

Parents have much to contribute to school (and therefore to children) in terms of enthusiasm, expertise and time. Nevertheless, there is another point of view which must not be forgotten: some parents, particularly perhaps those in more depressed, low-income areas, may have relatively little to offer – mainly because they themselves are in need of help and support. Adults who are deprived – either socially, emotionally or physically – have relatively few inner resources on which to draw, and are therefore relatively limited in their ability to offer help and support to others. It seems inappropriate to expect parents who are already burdened and, perhaps, depressed and deprived as well, to become involved in school activities which mean so much 'giving out' unless they themselves receive something in return.

In *family-systems* terms, systems function more effectively if all the members feel understood, respected and supported. In *practical* terms, it makes sense for schools to try to see that parents receive a measure of support – perhaps by providing them with a room of their own and coffee-making facilities; and the opportunity to talk to each other, and to staff, and perhaps to social workers, health visitors, psychologists and doctors if and when it seems appropriate.

The possibilities for using schools in these more open and flexible ways are enormous, particularly in infant and nursery schools where there is often a real opportunity for teachers to link up with parents for the benefit of children. Schools could be encouraged to hold discussion groups for parents on the needs of children and on parenting. (Some already do this, of course.) Parenting skills might be taught where this seemed appropriate, and good parent–child relationships fostered (see Bromwich, 1981; de'Ath, 1982). In other words, infant and nursery schools can be places where parents can both offer help, and receive it: both the giving and receiving will be of benefit to the children.

The role of the educational psychologist

It is probable that many educational psychologists are already involved in such school-based schemes in nursery and infant school, involving parents, teachers and children. Some of them have written about their involvement in workshops for handicapped children and children who are developmentally retarded (see Burton *et al.*, 1981; Moore *et al.*, 1981). However, the scope for this work is considerable and relevant to *all* infant and pre-school children and their families. In short, there are many parents who would welcome and benefit from the opportunity to discuss their children's developmental difficulties – transitory or fundamental, real or (partly) imagined – with a child psychologist.

It is suggested that a knowledge of family-systems theory is invaluable to the educational psychologist who undertakes such work. This knowledge includes an understanding of the various factors which create and maintain a family system, the various stresses and strains which may prevail within that system, and the way in which the different factors and processes can have a powerful influence on the young children at a very early age.

12

Learning difficulties

The term 'learning difficulties' can be applied to the performance of children with very different problems. We are here primarily concerned with children of average or above average intelligence, but whose performance falls well below the level of others of the same age group, rather than with children who have generalized learning problems (i.e. are 'globally' retarded or handicapped). Such children are sometimes described as having a specific learning disability, or as being dyslexic.

Although there are many different ways of describing, diagnosing and treating learning difficulties in intelligent children, they all tend to focus on the child's performance. That is to say, *maximum* attention is paid to what the child can and cannot do (in reading, spelling, or auditory or visual memory tests, for example) and *minimum* attention (if any) to his experience of himself as an individual, and to his relationships with others. In my view, this is quite a serious weakness in most, if not all, of the approaches. It is suggested that a child's learning difficulties, in common with all his activities and manifestations of his personality and intellect, normally bear some relationship to attitudes and communications which prevail within the child's family. This is not, of course, to suggest that his problems are caused directly by these attitudes – this would be altogether too simplistic a view of what is almost certainly an extremely complicated subject.

The child's symptoms and family attitudes

In Chapter 6 it was suggested that a child's learning problem may sometimes serve a purpose in the family system. The example given was that of a boy whose parents, on the point of divorce, were continually brought together to discuss his educational difficulties. It was felt that this state of affairs produced a situation where the boy had an interest in maintaining his 'symptoms' until he recognized that the separation of the parents had indeed taken place.

In my experience, it is not uncommon to find that the child has in some ways a vested interest in *not* learning – just as it is relatively common to find that family attitudes are tending to keep the child in the role of the 'one with the problem'. This attitude is usually characterized by a tendency to see, and to talk about, the child as though he were completely different from other children. Thus, instead of regarding him as being somewhat inferior to others in one area of functioning (e.g. reading) – but perhaps superior in other areas – the family tends to see him as being in a different category from other children (*he* is dyslexic, *others* are normal). There are many reasons why this state of affairs comes about: some parents may find it easier to come to terms with the child's difficulty if it has a label with a medical flavour; others may find it easier to focus on this one aspect of the child's development, rather than think about (for example) his social difficulties – or even their own matrimonial problems.

Considerable anxiety quite often surrounds the child's performance at reading and writing, although this may not necessarily be expressed directly by the parents. This anxiety, though entirely understandable, tends to create a tense atmosphere which is very unhelpful to the child. It may also result in well-meaning pressure from the parents. (This was the case in Peter's family, see below.)

Occasionally, parental attitudes towards reading are

ambivalent. This may be the case where a father cannot himself read, and feels threatened by the knowledge that his children are developing skills which will reveal his weakness. (Again, the parent may not necessarily admit to this. Even more dramatically, the parent may have kept his own weakness a secret from the children. This can be a difficult area, and one which the psychologist needs to approach with caution.) In cases where the child knows that father cannot read comfortably, he may himself feel uncertain about the prospect of learning to read. Is it 'safe' or acceptable, to learn a skill which your father does not have? The situation may be made even more uncertain if the 'women' of the family are good readers, and the 'men' (and boys) are not. Is reading a skill which is associated with masculinity or femininity? (This was the situation in the case of Mark, described below.)

It is not in any way suggested these family attitude factors are sufficient *in themselves* to make a child a non-reader, or to cause a specific learning disability in a child – many different factors and processes must contribute to this state of affairs. Nor is any criticism of the parents intended, since they are usually doing their best for the child and are not fully aware that a change of attitude might be appropriate. It *is* suggested though that the child benefits if the psychologist understands something of his experience within his own family system, and uses that knowledge sensitively as part of the overall strategy to help the child.

Two cases are given in an attempt to illustrate these points.

Peter

Peter, aged 8½, was referred with a severe difficulty in writing. In addition, he was described as having very poor concentration and some difficulty in his relationship with other children (he was somewhat aggressive and provocative). He was attending a well-run primary school, in a reasonably prosperous area. Peter read quite well (reading age eight years) but his written work was barely at the level of an average 6-year-old child in spelling, presentation and content. He was verbally competent, and usually knew the answers to questions in the classroom. However, when required to write, Peter always managed to procrastinate, to the annoyance of teachers and his parents.

Individual assessment Alone, Peter performed well on the Wechsler Intelligence Test, though scores for performance tests were lower than for the verbal tests (e.g. in the average and above average range respectively). This was regarded as rather less significant than the sentence-completion test, in which Peter gave indication of real anger towards his father.

Family interview Peter's parents were confused in their attitudes towards Peter, his work, and the school. They sought to blame the school for not teaching him at one moment, then changed to saying that he was lazy and difficult at the next. Later in the same conversation they said he was 'no trouble'. One thing was clearly apparent, however: Peter's father was putting considerable pressure on Peter. There was an older sister (13) doing very well at school with whom Peter had to compete.

When asked by the parents what was the 'matter' with Peter, and whether he was dyslexic, the psychologist replied that Peter had a problem with writing in that it was *more difficult* for him to write than it was for other children. She did not attempt to label this difficulty, but drew parallels with other human differences (e.g. in playing football, singing, sewing, etc.). At the same time, the psychologist made the point that Peter was an intelligent child, whom she did not see as lazy. She praised the father for his desire to help Peter, then asked if he would be prepared to forget about Peter's writing for a while himself, while she (the psychologist) tried certain interventions with Peter. The father agreed to this, though actually found it hard to stop pressurizing Peter. The topic needed to be re-introduced at each session.

It was suggested to the parents that the psychologist would:
- visit the school and make one or two suggestions to the teachers
- see Peter for individual weekly sessions for half a term
- meet with the parents after these sessions to keep in touch and discuss his progress.

Visit to school Peter's teacher was told that, although he definitely had a problem with writing, much of Peter's difficulties lay with his anxieties which were blocking his progress. She was asked if she could accept *less* work from Peter, but insist that it was well done. She was also asked to think of ways in which she could find situations to praise Peter whenever possible. Support from the school was good, and Peter was given merit marks for effort, which pleased him greatly.

Peter alone Peter had eight sessions with the psychologist, lasting three-quarters of an hour each, when he could choose his own activity from various creative materials (drawing, plasticine, sand and water). He was also encouraged to talk – which he did almost non-stop. His drawing was not very good but he modelled with enthusiasm, banging the clay and moulding it with angry movements and facial expressions. His conversation was mainly about his sister (who bullied him, according to Peter), the other children in school (who 'didn't like' him), and his parents. Considerable antagonism was expressed about them, though in a rather veiled manner. They favoured his sister, he thought, and were always nagging at him.

These sessions were used partly as an attempt to help Peter let off steam, and partly as counselling sessions. After listening to Peter's point of view for a while, the psychologist gradually introduced the idea that Peter himself might change (e.g. towards the other children at school).

Family sessions (two before and three after the individual sessions) The parents attended well, bringing both children with them. It soon became apparent that, far from being 'no trouble' at home, Peter was actually seen as annoying and provocative (of his sister), and lazy and rude to his parents. Peter, on the other hand, saw himself as a victim of his sister's teasing and bullying. The parents themselves were caring and intelligent people, but too strict and rather old-fashioned in their attitudes to the children. Both wanted them to have a good education, which they themselves had missed.

Much of the time was devoted to an exchange of views and opinions. The psychologist attempted to allow them all to express themselves on different subjects, while at the same time stepping in if one member of the family appeared to be at a disadvantage. Full recognition was made of the parents' desire to help their children. The father's ambition for Peter was praised before an attempt was made to suggest that perhaps the pressure might at times be too great for Peter – children, after all, pressurize themselves. Peter wanted to succeed, even though he sometimes appeared lazy and uncaring.

The children's relationship with each other was discussed, and it was suggested to the parents that arguments among children are normal. On the whole, parents do well not to interfere; nevertheless, certain rules do need to be made. Peter should not be allowed to go into his sister's room and interfere with her things. On the other hand, maybe he could occasionally be defended (as smaller and weaker) from her teasing and her sharp tongue?

Peter's performance gradually improved. More important, even, his attitude towards others improved. For the first time, he began to make real friends rather than take refuge in provocative, annoying behaviour towards other children at school.

Mark

Mark was referred to the school psychological service at the age of 7 years 9 months with severe difficulties in reading and, to a rather lesser extent, in writing. (This is perhaps a little unusual. Most children who have difficulty with reading have an even greater difficulty with writing.) The teacher commented that Mark was an intelligent boy who was falling behind the others in reading and writing. His behaviour in the classroom was described as good, though he showed a tendency to take refuge behind a winning smile rather than concentrate on his work. Teachers also commented that he showed some reluctance to join in with the activities of other children, and that he seemed rather too dependent on teachers at an age when this behaviour is largely outgrown.

Individual assessment Mark's performance in the WISC–R showed no difficulties in the area of perceptual performance. Scores for the different sub-tests were all within the high average range: reading age – 5.09 on the Holborn scale; writing – immature, with some reversals, mainly on b and d, and many spelling mistakes; drawing – immature, houses drawn with the windows tight to the corners and the chimneys at right-angles with the pitch of the roof, people drawn at about the 6-year-old level.

Conversation with Mark on his own and projective testing did not reveal anything that was of significance. He was pleasant, very talkative, with a good use of English, though a rather limited and immature choice of subject-matter. He had a very slight lisp.

Family diagnostic interview The whole family was invited to discuss Mark's difficulties, and the ways in which he might best be helped. The family consisted of father, mother, two sisters, aged 12 and 10 years, and Mark.

Mark's father was a rather tense-looking man who almost immediately admitted to his dislike of schools and teachers, and to his anger with the staff at Mark's school who had been unsuccessful in teaching Mark to read. A suggestion that he tell the psychologist about his own experience of schools and teachers as a boy led to a description of the father's own educational difficulties. He had not managed to learn and had left school barely able to read or write. (He was, however, successfully employed in a garage at the time of the interview.) Further exploration of the father's education experience revealed that part of the reason for his failure lay in the fact that his own father had kept him away from school to help in his business. His father had also been a violent man. Mark's father's conflicts could be described as: 'I loved my father, yet he hit me and kept me away from school' and 'I wanted to go to school, yet they couldn't teach me when I was there.' The conflicts were, at the time when Mark was going to school, expressed through anger directed at schools and teachers in general, which were seen to be failing Mark.

Mark's mother was a lively, intelligent and competent woman. She had had a grammar school education and enjoyed reading. During the diagnostic session she immediately showed a tendency to dominate, answer on behalf of others, and so on. She was a much more coherent and fluent talker than her husband. Her view of Mark was that he would 'manage'. Her real pride, however, lay in her older daughter who was doing very well at secondary school. Her attitude to her husband was placatory. She allowed him to explode, then stepped in after a while to dismiss him from the conversation with a smile.

Both sisters were talkative and friendly. The older girl was particularly powerful, showing a combination of general maturity and academic success at school.

During the diagnostic interview, Mark sat and smiled for most of the time. When asked a question by the psychologist, he showed no annoyance when either mother or the older sister answered (or tried to answer) on his behalf. He gave a strong feeling of a passive, 'cuddly' little boy who was being treated rather like a baby – or even an object, with no mind or will of his own.

It was apparent that the relationship between family members was quite good. They were a happy and intelligent family, though a closer look at the ways in which the members of the family reacted and responded to each other indicated areas of stress for Mark. It was a family in which the women seemed to be too powerful. Father kept his end up by the occasional angry outburst (for example, against schools) but this anger tended to be ignored or smoothed over by one or other of the women of the family. It was also apparent that Mark was being subjected to conflicting messages from the father: 'Schools are no good, and you can manage without teachers' versus 'You *must* learn to read'.

Areas of conflict for Mark might therefore be outlined as follows.

(1) I love Dad and want to be like him. He can't read and I am supposed to be able to read.
(2) Dad doesn't like schools. I like schools.
(3) My mother and sisters read and they are women. I want to be a man.

School visit Mark was already being given some individual help in a small group at school. The psychologist recommended that the teacher encourage him to write his own stories (with help) and to read them back. This made use of Mark's interest (and relative skill) in writing as a foundation for reading. It was also suggested that Mark be encouraged to make choices and decisions for himself, and to take certain responsibilities that would help him develop a more positive attitude.

Family sessions The psychologist felt that Mark's father's ambivalence towards education and his bitterness at his own failure were important factors, and she therefore allowed the father plenty of time to talk about himself in the family sessions. She sympathized with him, then moved towards discussing those things which he did well (e.g. practical things).

The psychologist also brought into the open the idea that reading might be a 'feminine' skill, and suggested that while it was true that some boys tended to be slower off the mark than girls at reading, most of them caught up and read equally competently eventually.

The conversation was then directed to competence generally – the competence of Mark and his father in particular. Reading was put in its place, as a useful skill, but not necessarily all-important – after all, Mark's father had managed quite well without it over the years.

It was noticeable that Mark's mother and sisters tended to answer for him. Also that they tended to laugh at him when he answered for himself. He didn't seem to mind this – seemed to take it for granted – but the psychologist made the point of *not* laughing, and of encouraging him to answer for himself. She then listened attentively and seriously to his replies.

Four family sessions were held in all. Mark began to make progress in reading at school, though he is still rather immature and lacking in drive. It was felt that further intervention would be inappropriate.

Concluding comments

In my view, it is always helpful to pay some attention to the family dynamics when a child has a specific learning difficulty. It is not, however, suggested that these sessions 'cure' the problem, but rather that they form part of the overall strategy to help the child.

In some ways, it might seem that parents would find it hard

to understand why they should meet the psychologist for four or five sessions when the problem is, or appears to be, exclusively educational. In fact, parents seem to accept and even enjoy such sessions. Presumably the opportunity to discuss with the psychologist other things which worry them (e.g. the child's behaviour at home, as in Peter's case; their own unresolved conflicts, as in the case of Mark's father) is helpful to them. And it is surprising how often there *are* other problems in the family. Whatever the reason, in my experience parents of children with problems, such as those experienced by Peter and Mark, attend well, with few broken appointments.

It is recognized that this work is limited in many ways to certain types of children from certain types of family background (i.e. relatively intelligent children from relatively supportive and intelligent families). Also that heavy caseloads may well prevent psychologists from undertaking it. Nevertheless, it can be very rewarding; equally, it can be preventative of more serious problems. In the case of Peter, for example, it seems probable that his poor attitudes to his work and to other children and adults could have led to quite serious difficulties in adolescence.

13

Counselling in a family-systems framework

Many educational psychologists undertake counselling sessions with individual children (usually adolescents) as part of their work with schools and school children. Sometimes a psychologist undertakes individual sessions with a child over a period of time, with a view to helping him overcome certain social or behavioural difficulties. At other times, counselling takes place once or twice only with more limited goals – perhaps as part of the process of assessment and diagnosis undertaken to understand the child more fully.

The psychologist will often be aware, or will become aware, that there are problems in the child's family. It is also quite common for educational psychologists to find that other professionals (social workers, psychiatrists, probation officers) are involved either with the child's family as a whole, or with other family members: for example, the family may be receiving family therapy in the child psychiatric department of a local hospital, or the mother may be receiving psychiatric treatment in a day unit, or long-term help from a social worker. Once the psychologist is aware that other professionals are involved with the child or his family it is important to work closely with them to establish a co-ordinated approach to helping the child. (The difficulties of team work in helping children are discussed in Murgatroyd, 1980. See also Chapter 17.)

Quite often, however, there is no one else involved with a referred child whom a psychologist is counselling. She will know relatively little about the child except (almost certainly) that he is constantly in trouble at school. Although it is quite possible to take this as a starting-point for counselling a referred child, the psychologist might well feel that a meeting with the child's parents would also be useful. The aims of this meeting would be to (a) obtain certain information about the child's past experience from the parents; (b) make some assessment of the parental personalities and of the family system; and (c) obtain parental support for the counselling sessions.

It is probably most appropriate for a family meeting to take place with the psychologist *before* the counselling sessions are started. Indeed, the meeting can act as a valuable starting point to understanding and helping the child. However, it is possible to meet the child's parents after the sessions have been in progress for a while, though in this case the psychologist needs to obtain the child's permission before meeting the parents. It is recognized that there are many complex ethical and legal implications here. It is assumed that parents have given their permission for the psychologist to see their child. Once the psychologist has formed a relationship with the child, and received information from him given on a basis of trust and confidence, it seems inappropriate for the psychologist to approach the child's parents without discussing this fully with him beforehand. (These, and other issues of confidentiality and commitment, are discussed more fully by Murgatroyd, 1980, and by Noonan, 1983.)

In the following case, counselling was undertaken with a child whose parents were reluctant to co-operate with the psychologist on a regular basis. They were seen for an initial interview, then at the end of the six counselling sessions offered to the child.

Jamie

Jamie, aged 13, was referred with behavioural difficulties at school. He was described as devious and provocative of other children, and rude to staff. His work was poor, and frequently unfinished. He had been suspended twice from school.

Jamie's father and mother came with him for the interview at the request of the psychologist. His father spent most of the time criticizing the school and the school staff, while his mother criticized Jamie's behaviour at home. Much of the interview was spent (for the psychologist) in listening, and certain important information was gradually revealed.

Jamie was living with his father and stepmother, his own mother having left home when he was about 7. It appeared that his relationship with his stepmother was not too good, and that his father (though defending him during the interview with the psychologist) was actually quite hard on him. He had a 4-year-old stepsister, who appeared to be doted on by everyone in the family.

When the psychologist mentioned the possibility of a second family interview the father began to make difficulties, and to explain that his working hours made visits to the psychologist difficult. It also seemed unlikely that the stepmother would be sufficiently committed to attending regular sessions, so Jamie was offered individual counselling sessions at the end of the school day. All the family agreed to this.

Jamie was an attractive, anxious boy, very eager to please and to say and do the right things. He had set very high standards for himself at home in an attempt to live up to his father's expectations – and not to fall foul of his stepmother. The effort was too great, and the result was a tendency to let go from time to time and indulge in rude and provocative behaviour. Since he found it impossible to recognize this 'bad' aspect of his personality, Jamie also spent a considerable amount of time deceiving others and shifting the blame whenever possible.

At first, Jamie was defensive about himself and his weaknesses. The psychologist made it easier for him by talking about the things he had done in a relaxed and accepting manner, while at the same time commenting that she knew he was not a bad person and probably did not really intend to do the things which got him into trouble. She encouraged him to talk about himself and about his friends and various activities, spending most of the first session listening to him.

At the second session, the psychologist asked Jamie about his mother whom he had not seen since she left home. He 'didn't know' why she had left, but knew that she had married someone else. He remembered her 'quite well', and spoke of her without bitterness. Nevertheless, it was clear that he was confused about her and about the reasons why she had left him and his father.

Jamie was guarded on the subject of his stepmother, and the subject was dropped. He said he liked his stepsister, but smiled with relief when the psychologist commented that she must be rather a nuisance at times. Details of the way in which she made things difficult were then given: changing channels during favourite television programmes, staying up late and talking all the time, crying if he got cross with her. It was also apparent that he was frequently required to baby-sit while his father and stepmother went out at the weekends.

Speaking of his father, Jamie said he was 'all right', but a bit strict. He got on 'quite well' with him. He didn't see very much of him since he was a driver and therefore went away a lot.

The six individual counselling sessions allowed Jamie to off-load some of his more negative feelings towards his family (particularly his stepsister). They also gave the psychologist the opportunity to talk about school, and his relationship with other pupils and with members of staff. It was recognized openly (by the psychologist) that some lessons *are* boring; also that it is sometimes difficult to keep one's temper when teachers get cross, or other children behave in a provocative manner. Nevertheless, one had to try.

During the last session, it was suggested to Jamie that it

might be a good idea if his parents and stepsister came again. He was told that it was not the psychologist's intention to tell them things that *they* had discussed together, but it might be helpful if they did all meet, so that the psychologist could hear how things were at home. Jamie agreed to this, though without much enthusiasm.

The family session was difficult to arrange and many excuses were made by the parents about why attendance was 'impossible'. The psychologist also had to overcome certain negative feelings of her own about Jamie's father and stepmother. It seemed unreasonable to her that they could not find time to attend a meeting to help Jamie without a great deal of complex negotiation. Finally, an early evening appointment was made.

In many ways, an interview with the child's parents after individual counselling sessions have taken place is more difficult than an interview beforehand. Inevitably a bond has been forged between child and psychologist during the counselling sessions, and the psychologist may identify with the child to the point of not being able to see the parental viewpoint. In Jamie's case there *was* a parental viewpoint – that he often was rather rude and difficult – with which the psychologist was able to sympathize.

Two important factors came out of the family interview. First, a discussion of Jamie's stepsister was undertaken, and the parents were able to recognize that they relied on Jamie for baby-sitting, and that at times a 4-year-old child might be a nuisance to an adolescent boy. Secondly, the psychologist was able to ask about Jamie's natural mother. The father talked about her with a certain degree of bitterness. It was clear that he regarded the matter as being finished with, belonging to the past, though he could see that Jamie might occasionally be curious about his natural mother.

During this session, the psychologist became aware that the stepmother had some difficulty in coming to terms with her more negative feelings about Jamie. Although he looked at her constantly for approval, she tended to look away from him and out of the window. It was possible to feel some sympathy for her as a woman who had tried to meet the needs of another woman's child for whom she apparently felt no maternal affection. The psychologist therefore made the point that it must have been difficult for her to take on a child when she had been quite young herself.

Jamie was seen once again alone after this session. He seemed more settled at school, and was not getting into trouble as often as before. His work had improved. Little was said in that session, but the psychologist was given the impression that Jamie felt considerably happier about himself and his school work.

It is suggested that this method of seeing the family before the counselling sessions start and after they have finished has considerable advantages. It is very helpful for the psychologist to see the family and to get a view of the child as part of his family system. The initial session also allows for some fact-finding. The psychologist has the opportunity to begin the therapeutic process by bringing about some slight shift in the family dynamics. In the case of Jamie, for example, the initial interview gave the parents a chance to express some of their negative feelings, which might otherwise have been directed at Jamie. It also allowed everyone to feel that 'something was being done' – a feeling which can of itself bring about some improvement in the behaviour of individuals in a family.

A final session with the family at the end of the counselling sessions is also useful. Although the psychologist needs to be aware of the possibility of having identified somewhat with the child during the individual sessions, a final session does give her the opportunity to 'hand back' the child to the family, and to leave the door open for them to contact her again should the need arise.

14

Joint systems: psychologist, family and school

Children are part of, and influenced by, two important systems: family and school. Their behaviour and performance reflect experiences, both past and present, within these two systems. Equally and simultaneously, the child's own actions and attitudes exert a powerful influence on both systems, for better or worse. At the same time, certain factors and communications *between* the two systems can sometimes have a powerful influence on the way in which the child behaves.

A joint-systems approach to helping children overcome behavioural difficulties, and problems associated with their development, is undertaken when the practitioner's work with a knowledge of the child and of *both systems* which include the child. This approach differs from the traditional child guidance model where people work as part of a team, taking a separate and clearly defined role: social worker (for the parents), psychologist (for the child in school), psychotherapist (for the child in treatment), and psychiatrist (as diagnostician of the child and perhaps as decision-maker). In this model, the contribution of each professional is based on *one* perspective of the total problem. Such an approach can be valuable, but it can also founder on misunderstanding, as well as being extremely expensive in terms of man hours.

In the joint-systems approach, the practitioners have an understanding both of the child as an individual and of the two systems in which the child operates. The approach is not necessarily new. Indeed, it probably forms part of the repertoire of many educational psychologists (and others), attempting to help children overcome behavioural difficulties at school. It is, however, poorly documented and apparently unevaluated as a technique for helping children. Although there are many reasons for the lack of literature on the subject, an important factor must be its relative complexity – as a subject for discussion that is.

Commenting on a joint-systems approach it is necessary to take into consideration, at one and the same time, at least six different factors:

(a) the child himself with all his observable strengths and weaknesses
(b) the family as a system
(c) the school as a system
(d) interactions between (a), (b) and (c)
(e) the role of the psychologist and her relationship with the systems and with individuals in the systems
(f) occasional overriding factors such as the need for a child to be taken into care, on the sudden departure of a parent.

This chapter looks at some of these factors, and considers the ways in which a joint-systems approach can be used for the benefit of children who are failing at school. It is suggested that the approach has a wide application, though, in common with any other treatment method, it has its disadvantages as well as its advantages.

Family-systems theory and the school system

Although educational psychologists have a good understanding of schools, and are accustomed to intervening in the school system (see Gillham, 1978) it is arguable that they have paid insufficient attention to studying the more subtle and dynamic processes that make up *any* social system. Tucker and Dyson (1966) describe the school as having many of the characteristics of a family system. Whereas there should be a degree of mutual respect between members of the system, and clear boundaries of functioning between the different sub-systems, more negative factors may in fact upset and unbalance the system. Jealousies and rivalries between individuals and between departments, poor communication between adults, feelings of despair and confusion, can all result in unsatisfactory staff attitudes to a child with problems. Each individual adult may be doing his best by his own lights, yet subtle factors in the system are producing stress – which in turn adversely affects the child.

The effects of ignoring these more subtle, and sometimes quite destructive, aspects of a school system can be considerable. It is unrealistic to imagine that the psychologist's recommendations will always be well received by teachers. A particular teacher may, for example, dislike the psychologist, or the senior member of staff who has asked her to carry out the psychologist's recommendations. Alternatively, a teacher may have been led to believe that the child would be removed from the school, and must now come to terms with the fact that he is not going, and that *she* must devote time and energy to a special programme to help the child. These problems are not insurmountable, but they cannot be ignored since they can be the cause of failure in an otherwise well-planned scheme.

It is suggested that the family-systems ideas and theories that have been described in previous chapters can be applied equally in schools. These include recognizing that:

(1) the child's behaviour often reflects an unsatisfactory adult–child system, based often on negative attitudes on *both* sides, and a 'stuck' or rigid relationship
(2) the adult (teacher) cannot be co-opted as a partner with the psychologist (i.e. to apply certain techniques to the child) unless the psychologist also pays attention to the nature of the teacher–child system
(3) the needs of viewpoint of everyone must be taken into

consideration – as in family therapy, attempts to intervene on the child's behalf without considering the adult's viewpoint are likely to fail

(4) certain subtle factors in the relationship between parents and teachers may be conspiring to keep the child's symptoms 'alive'

(5) certain factors in the relationship between the psychologist and one or more of the individuals may be unhelpful from the point of view of help for the child.

Child, family and school

Children gain their view of the world and of others primarily from their parents. The child's perception of his teachers, and his attitude towards them, will be strongly influenced by his experience of his parents – both in the past, and on a day-to-day basis. If the child's experience of adults at home is that they are sensible, competent and caring, he is likely to respond positively to his teachers. If his experience is that adults are confusing, punishing, unpredictable and easily manipulated, he will react to teachers accordingly. Sometimes the child's view of adults corresponds with what they really are, sometimes it does not. A child who has cause to link wrong-doing with rejection and violence at home may experience a teacher's mild rebuke as dislike or rejection of him as an individual. Gentleness and kindness on the part of the teacher may be experienced (initially at least) as 'softness' by a child who has not had the opportunity to learn that kindness and discipline can coexist. (Of course, some teachers actually *are* rejecting, or 'soft' in their attitudes towards children.)

Children can easily be confused by a direct conflict of attitudes between adults. They may, for example, be expected to conform to rules in school which the parents claim openly to despise. Not only is this lack of consensus between adults confusing for the child, it may encourage him to play off one system against the other, exploiting adult disagreement to his own short-term satisfaction.

Children quite often (and, one might say, quite naturally) try to create certain situations at school which are familiar to them at home. The child may feel that these situations are to his advantage, although they often unfortunately lead to his downfall. On the other hand, some children are so immature and confused that it is both impossible and unrealistic to suggest that they *deliberately* set up situations. These are children who respond automatically and without forethought, in any way which seems to them to be appropriate at the moment, even if it is disastrous in the long term. They resort regularly to quick and angry responses or to violent acts or telling lies in an attempt to evade the consequences of their actions. They are unable to control and direct their behaviour, and need help if they are to be able to achieve a measure of self-control and self-respect.

Parents and the school

Teachers and parents are part of the same society and will, up to a point at least, have the same expectations, hopes and understanding of the children in their charge. Thus they will all want the best for the child, according to his needs and abilities. They will also – in theory at least – be in broad agreement that certain forms of behaviour are unacceptable, and that some degree of discipline is needed. Nevertheless, there are areas of potential disagreement between parents and school, some of which are justified, and some of which are the outcome of confused attitudes or anxiety and anger in either parent, school or both. Disagreements between parents and school are likely to arise over such questions as:

Is the child being appropriately taught?
Does he have a *real* learning or behavioural problem?
Is he underachieving, or lacking in ability?

Which behaviour is really unacceptable?
How should unacceptable behaviour be handled?

Parents' attitudes to school and to teachers depend partly on their own experience in education in the past, and partly on their belief in themselves as competent and acceptable individuals. Parents who have had a reasonably good experience of schools in their own childhood, and have a confident and realistic view of themselves and of their children, are usually content to let teachers get on with the job of teaching, giving their support as and when it is needed. Such parents are not usually guilty of over-pressurizing their children, or of over-reacting when things go wrong. If problems occur, they are able to take a realistic view of the situation, and co-operate with the school for the benefit of the child.

Nevertheless, it must be recognized that at times the child's behaviour and/or performance at school places both parents and teachers under strain. Children who behave unpredictably – for whatever reason – can arouse considerable antagonism in adults which often results in defensive and angry attitudes. Thus, in Roe's (1978) words, children dig themselves into holes, and adults keep them there.

Bridging the gaps between family and school

The psychologist who knows both the family of a referred child and the school which the child attends is in a good position to help the child by bridging any gaps which may exist between the attitudes of staff and those of the child's parents. This can be done either at a joint interview (psychologist, teachers and parents), or at separate interviews. In the latter case, the psychologist bears in mind the needs and attitudes of *both* parties during the separate interviews.

The gaps – real or imagined – that exist between a child's parents and his teachers usually come about for several reasons, which can be summarized as: (a) differing viewpoints of the same problem; and (b) adult anxiety and defensiveness when faced with a problem which might seem at first sight insoluble.

Differing viewpoints between teachers and parents

Parents and teachers, though they usually all have the welfare of the child at heart, often have a very different understanding of the same problem. Parents do not appreciate the pressures associated with maintaining school discipline, nor the difficulties that face a class teacher who must try to meet the needs of thirty or so children, all of whom have different needs and different abilities. Teachers, on the other hand, are often unaware of the domestic or personal problems that face the families of the children they teach. There is a tendency for both sides to behave as though certain things 'should be so'. The parent thinks that the teacher 'should be able to' teach or control the child, however difficult the child is. The teacher, on the other hand, thinks that the child 'should be able to' conform, or learn, and that the parents 'should be able to' discipline the child so that he does his homework, attends school regularly, and so on. When things go wrong, there is a strong tendency for each party to blame the other, and to take refuge in increasingly defensive and angry attitudes. The gap tends to widen, unfortunately, unless help can be offered.

It is the task of the psychologist, therefore, to allow for a certain clearing of the air while at the same time bringing the sides together a little. A careful balancing act takes place as each side is encouraged to recognize and admit to the possibility that the other might have a point of view. (Not, it is noted, that the other side might be *right*, merely that there is more than one way of looking at things.)

Adult anxiety

Symptomatic (i.e. unusual, destructive or immature) behaviour in children is quite often a source of great anxiety to adults, who tend to feel instinctively that they should be able to control the child and do something about his behaviour. Understandable as these attitudes are, they often result in an increase in the child's symptoms as the adult tightens his control – often inappropriately – on the child. It is important, therefore, that none of the adults feels a unique obligation to change the child. In other words, that none of the adults should feel blamed, or pressurized, either by the other party, or by the psychologist.

In my view, it is important to recognize that:

(a) the child does have a problem
(b) the child actually wants to overcome his problem, though it may not always look like it
(c) the psychologist will work with the parents and the school in an attempt to help the child
(d) there are no quick answers or magic cures.

The joint interview

Joint interviews with teachers, parents and psychologist (and perhaps the child as well) are valuable in that they allow for an important and direct exchange of views between all parties (see Hurford, 1983). On the other hand, they can be stressful to some or all of the participants and, at worst, deteriorate into an unhelpful or chaotic situation. The psychologist needs to feel confident either of her ability to take the lead in a joint interview (see Aponte, 1976), or at least to orchestrate the different viewpoints. This may be a formidable task in the case of some families, particularly where there is a long-standing history of behavioural disturbance in the child, around which adult attitudes have tended to harden. Arguably, the psychologist should only undertake a joint interview if she feels confident to do so. If not, it is possible to hold separate interviews and bring about a similar *rapprochement* between the adults.

In the case described below, one joint interview was arranged, followed by two family interviews and a further discussion with the school a few weeks later.

Olivia

Olivia, aged 7, was referred after two years in infant school during which she had made very little progress. The only child of relatively elderly parents, she tended to cling to her father in the playground and to cry when he left her. In the classroom she usually kept apart from others, refusing to join in or to take part in any activity. Very occasionally she settled to a task, and produced a lively drawing or read aloud to the teacher. It was felt that she would be lost in the junior school without the support and encouragement of her infant class teacher.

Olivia was quite an intelligent child, although her school work did not reflect this. On the Wechsler Intelligence Test there was a marked scatter of sub-test scores. She was particularly poor on verbal comprehension, and seemed to have no idea what one should do in certain simple situations.

Teachers at school felt that Olivia was over-protected by her parents. Her clinging to her father tended to support this view, as did Olivia's poor understanding of some of the basic rules of life in the verbal comprehension test.

A joint interview between the parents, the headteacher and the psychologist was arranged. The parents were given time to discuss their anxieties about Olivia, and to question the headteacher and the psychologist. They were told that she was a bright little girl, who seemed to be lacking in confidence. Since they were obviously very anxious about her, reassurance seemed very important.

Towards the end of the interview, it was suggested to the father that it would be better if he brought Olivia just before school started, handed her to the teacher and left directly rather than hovering for a while to see if she was all right. At that point it was learnt that the father had recently been made redundant, a point which the psychologist felt needed discussing at a later date.

Later, the psychologist met with the parents and Olivia away from the school, and was able to ask a little more about the child, and the past history. She had been a premature infant, long-awaited. Though a sturdy, healthy little girl, her parents seemed unable to believe in her ability to survive without them (or, perhaps, their own ability to survive without her).

There were feeding problems at home. Olivia tended to rule the roost, staying up late and coming into her parents' bedroom when she wanted to. The parents were depressed at the father's lack of a job (though they were not financially insecure), and Olivia seemed at times to be playing the role of comforter to her parents. These and other matters were discussed with Olivia and her parents over two or three meetings in an attempt to encourage (a) the parents to strengthen their attitudes towards Olivia, (b) Olivia to develop her own sense of identity, and (c) the parents to look towards developing their own relationship with each other (outings, clubs, etc.).

A further meeting between school and psychologist took place a few weeks later. Olivia was beginning to respond more normally, and to play with other children. She no longer clung to her father at the school gates. Perhaps even more important, the parents had begun to make contact with some of Olivia's classmates, and to invite them to play with her after school.

15

Joint systems and school refusal

It is perhaps in cases of persistent non-attendance that a psychologist can derive the greatest benefit from a joint-systems approach. A real understanding of the child's behaviour in terms of the processes that prevail in his family *and* of the system that prevails in the school often allows for effective action to be taken to re-integrate a child into mainstream education who might otherwise have needed special provision.

Before discussing this in some detail, however, it is necessary both to define non-attendance, and to mention certain limiting factors which might prevent the psychologist from bringing the child back into mainstream education. Much has been written about non-attendance, and many attempts made to place children in categories (truants, school phobics, etc.) as a preliminary to offering appropriate help. This, in my view, is a difficult undertaking, since there are many different factors and processes operating, some of which are only partly understood.

It is probable that non-attenders can more usefully be placed on a continuum, rather than allocated to a category. At one end of the continuum is the highly anxious and disturbed child, who develops extreme psychosomatic symptoms at the thought of school attendance; at the other end is the truant who fits in quite happily when at school, but simply prefers not to attend. In between these two extremes lie the vast majority of non-attenders. They often live in depressing circumstances at home; they sometimes have difficulties with school work, or with relationships with other children. They are sometimes bound by ties of dependency to depressed and anxious mothers. There may well be no motivation on the part of parents to get the child to school, or there may be double messages to the child: 'Go to school!' versus 'It's not safe to leave me!'

Regardless of the fundamental nature of the child's non-attendance difficulties, it is almost always the case that missing school tends to be rewarding in so far as it is both anxiety-reducing and, quite often, pleasurable in itself. If the child can 'get away with it' over a period of time, re-integration becomes quite difficult.

The psychologist's ability to re-integrate a child into school after a period of non-attendance, or spasmodic attendance, while at the same time working with the family will depend on several factors, largely beyond the psychologist's control. Though in a sense these factors are almost self-evident, they must be stated if an over-simplification of the problem is to be avoided. These factors include:

(1) the degree of anxiety experienced by the child (if any)
(2) the length of time the child has been out of school before being seen
(3) parental co-operation with the psychologist and school
(4) degree of flexibility/understanding within the school system
(5) the age of the child, and the nature of his peer group.

It is undoubtedly the case that good parental co-operation and an understanding school are essential factors in re-integrating children, particularly when the child's non-attendance is associated with some degree of anxiety. It is also, unfortunately, the case that children past the age of 14, who are failing in school as well as not attending regularly, are more difficult to help than younger children – particularly if the home background is chaotic, disturbed or uncaring. Older school children who have links with friends, perhaps older than they, who do not attend school will also be very difficult to re-integrate.

There may well be one or two factors within the school which are acting as genuine stumbling-blocks to re-integration for the child. Indeed, the child may see them as the *reason* for his non-attendance. While the psychologist must take this with a grain of salt, it cannot be denied that certain people, and certain lessons, may be difficult for the child to cope with. Although it is not suggested that children should be protected indefinitely from the realities of life, including disagreeable teachers and games lessons, it is obviously unhelpful it the non-attending child is placed in a disliked or feared situation immediately after re-integration.

Successful re-integration often depends on the child being received by a friendly member of staff when he returns to school, someone who is prepared to spend time talking to him and discussing the day's timetable with him. Children who have been out of school for some time are often faced with timetable changes when they return, as well as with the reality of having missed a considerable amount of schooling. Ideally, the member of staff should have close links with the psychologist, and be able to arrange for the child to avoid, temporarily, certain situations which the psychologist knows will almost certainly be stressful for the child. Where there is a school counsellor, he or she can usually undertake this role better than a class teacher, who is often under pressure from other sources and cannot give enough time to talking to the child. Nevertheless, teachers can perform this link-up task successfully. Perhaps the most important factor is that they be known to, and liked by, the child, and seen as a person to be approached if and when difficulties arise (as they almost certainly will).

Occasionally a non-attending child will set his heart on going to another school. The second school may be seen, either by the child or the parents or both, as the answer to the child's difficulties. In many cases, of course, this is a delusion, since the child tends to take his problems with him and quite often fails to attend the second school, perhaps after a brief honeymoon period. However, if a change of schools is proposed – or even insisted upon – the psychologist can agree to support child and family if this change is felt to be reasonably appropriate, while at the same time letting the family know that this may not necessarily be the answer to the child's difficulties. The family can then be offered sessions to help the child over the transition period, and the psychologist can make appropriate links with the new school. On the other hand, the psychologist may at times feel the need to stand firmly against the idea of a change of school, using this as a starting-point for a discussion of the child's problems in a more general sense. In other words, the psychologist needs to avoid the possibility of colluding with a child who has many social and emotional difficulties and who seeks to find a solution to his problems in the 'perfect' school.

Jason

Jason, aged 12, was referred early in his second term at secondary school, with an increasing number of absences from school. During the first term he had apparently found it difficult to get to school and had had several absences 'feeling ill'. After the Christmas break, he found it almost impossible to stay in school. His mother had developed the habit of taking him to school, waiting anxiously in the corridor for a while, then going home again. Jason frequently left school mid-morning or lunch time to go home to his mother. He would then refuse to go back again.

Family diagnostic interview The family was invited to a session to discuss Jason's difficulties. The family consisted of:
Father, in his late 30s. A thin, tense man whose manner indicated a certain lack of confidence.

Mother (late 30s). A rather solid and apparently confident woman.

Alison (17). A pleasant, outspoken girl.

Jason (12). Thin, anxious and with bitten nails, and a fleeting smile.

Sara (6). A rather chirpy little girl, with immature speech.

As soon as the family was assembled, certain patterns and alliances could be seen almost immediately. Father and Alison sat next to each other, and father continually made contact with Alison throughout the interview, looking at her and smiling at her. Mother and Jason sat next to each other, and Jason referred all his answers to the psychologist's questions to her ('. . . didn't we, Mum?'). Sara seemed a little apart from the others. Eye contact, and direction of gaze was very interesting:

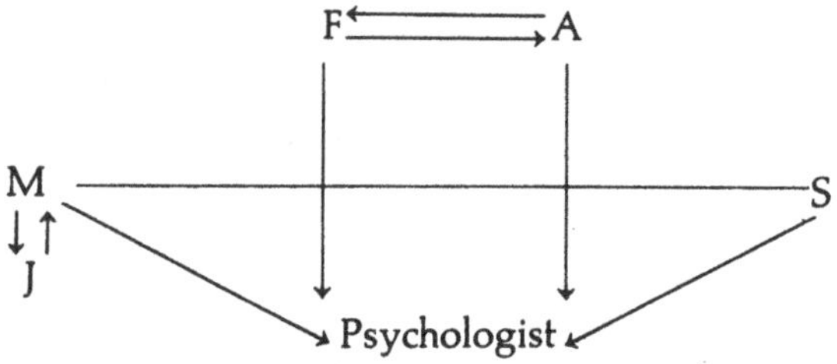

(a) Everyone – except Jason – looked at the psychologist from time to time.
(b) Jason always looked at mother.
(c) Father and Alison constantly exchanged glances.
(d) Mother and father didn't look at each other.

The family's hierarchy and the sub-systems could be drawn as:

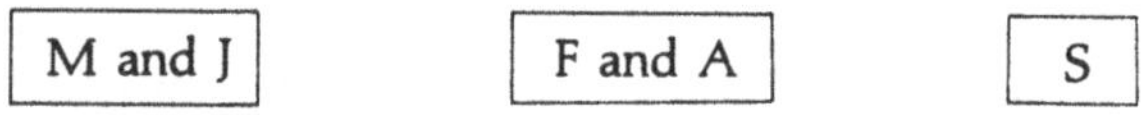

Mother was definitely the more powerful of the two parents, with the father a pleasant but relatively ineffectual person. Further investigation revealed a pattern of competent females running the family system: the maternal grandmother was also a very powerful woman, and Alison was a competent, mature girl. It could be said that the family belief system included the view that women were the strong ones.

It appeared that Jason and his mother had a close and anxious relationship. Such a tie is commonly found in children who have acute difficulty in attending school. It is as though neither mother nor child can believe in their ability to survive without each other (or perhaps believe in the ability of the other to survive without them). The feeling is mutual, and self-fuelling in a circular fashion: parental anxiety $\longleftrightarrow$ child's anxiety.

As is often the case in families where the boy is closely attached to the mother, the parental pair-bond appeared to be somewhat weak. The mother seemed to need her close relationship with Jason, who had to some extent replaced her husband as a source of emotional satisfaction. Father's own personality was an important factor in maintaining Jason's 'symptom'. He lacked the strength to send Jason off to school with confidence, and to break into the mother–child bond. At the same time it was difficult for Jason to identify with, and draw strength from, a father who was a relatively unsatisfactory masculine model. Yet Jason *needed* that identification if he was to be able to leave his mother's apron strings.

The focus of the therapy was on:

(1) understanding the individual needs, strengths and weaknesses of family members
(2) challenging (indirectly) the family's view
 (a) that Jason couldn't survive without mother
 (b) that women are invariably competent, dominant, etc.
 (c) that men are less competent and worthwhile than women.

It was felt that the spouses were not actually making realistic recognition of each other's strengths and weaknesses. For example, father was quite competent as a handyman, and an excellent cook (once he managed to get started). Mother was often tired and overburdened – a fact which father ignored.

The therapist spent some time talking to the parents individually – sympathizing with the mother for the household chores which she had to combine with a job, and showing interest in the father's cooking and handyman activities. She also paid attention to Jason, speaking to him directly and encouraging him to answer for himself. This was actually quite difficult. Though he did answer, it was by constant reference to the mother. Interestingly, this was the direct opposite of the father–daughter position, where *father* constantly referred to *daughter*. In both cases, however, it appeared to be the women who were the ones in the position of power, to be deferred to.

Jason was encouraged to talk about school in both its positive and negative aspects. He said he 'didn't mind it' once he was there, though he disliked certain lessons. He was encouraged to talk about the lessons he *disliked* while the psychologist showed sympathy. This was felt to be important. Jason's parents (like many parents whose children complain about school) had discouraged all negative attitudes ('You don't really mind ...') towards school, while at the same time expressing great anxiety that he *did* mind. The psychologist was very matter-of-fact about this – of course some lessons and some teachers could be boring and hard to bear. It was a pity, but that was life and everyone felt the same way. (This comment was aimed at decreasing anxiety in *all* members of the family.) Parents were encouraged to talk about their own feelings for school, both positive and negative.

Conversation was extended to more general topics. The psychologist asked Jason and his father what they did together as the 'men of the family'. It was apparent that they were both uneasy at the suggestion they might get together. (It would have been possible to set a task here, e.g. that father and son go fishing or to a football match together.) The mother and daughters were also encouraged to talk a bit about what they did together.

Contact with the school The psychologist contacted a member of staff at school known to be liked by, and sympathetic to, Jason. This teacher was asked to look out for Jason each morning and take him from his mother – sending the mother firmly away from the school in a friendly manner with the comment that the teacher would look after him and that mother need not worry. The teacher then spent ten minutes with Jason, making sure he knew exactly what was expected of him, where he was supposed to be, and so on.

After two family sessions Jason's re-integration in the school seemed complete. However, he started to drift away from school again at the beginning of the second year, so that a further intervention was planned. It was felt that one of the reasons that Jason found the second year difficult was that he was no longer in the care of a rather motherly tutor, but of a much sterner and more remote man. It seemed to the psychologist that this change was the cause of his anxiety. He seemed to have made use of the motherly characteristics of the first-year tutor to bridge the gap between his own mother and school. The male tutor was not able to fulfil this role, and Jason was insufficiently 'detached' from mother figures to allow him to identify with the male model. The intervention took two forms.

(1) The first-year tutor was asked if she could be breifly involved again as an anchor point, talking to Jason about his timetable, giving him five minutes of her time in the morning.
(2) The family was invited back to the clinic. After three sessions, during which Jason was allowed to express freely his own anxieties about being in the second year, and the parents encouraged to take a firmer approach, Jason was

successfully re-integrated. He attended the rest of the term without a break. Now in his third year, Jason's attendance remains good.

16

Parents and children from different cultural backgrounds

Psychologists have been reluctant, at least in recent years, to comment publicly on the learning difficulties and behavioural disturbance of children whose cultural background is not English, or to make comparisons between them and their English peers. This is particularly true in the field of educational and psychological research, where statistical data on children's performances can so easily be misinterpreted or misquoted to reinforce racial stereotypes, or even to provoke racist attitudes which might be harmful to individuals or to groups.

In spite of this reticence, many educational psychologists must have considerable experience of children and families whose cultural background differs from their own. The proportion of non-English children in some schools is very high, and inevitably a certain number of them will show signs of disturbed behaviour and/or learning difficulties – problems that are not, on the whole, very different from those exhibited by their English peers. Psychologists meeting every day with such children know how important it is to take into consideration some of the influnces of the child's background while at the same time treating him the same as an English child.

The two largest groups of children of non-English extraction are West Indian and Asian children. Within these two large groups are several sub-groups. When one speaks of an Asian community, it is in some ways like speaking of a European community. The group has certain common cultural characteristics but it also has characteristics associated with the smaller groupings of nationality, religion, class, etc. I have found working with families of West Indian or Asian background an interesting, though challenging and sometimes frustrating experience. Interesting, because of the fascination of seeing both similarities and differences between oneself and the parents of the referred child, and because a discussion with the parents of their ways of living and their experiences in England are often illuminating and thought-provoking; difficult and challenging because of the barriers of language and culture which can confuse or blur the issues one wishes to discuss. Some of the difficulties are practical (e.g. Do they understand what I am saying?), others more subtle. How, for example, do the parents of a referred child understand the role of a psychologist (a difficult enough task for English parents at times)? What family pressures and influences might be making difficulties for the referred child, which the psychologist, from the basis of her own cultural background, cannot know or understand? Can one ever attribute some, or all, of the child's 'symptoms' to cultural factors, language difficulties, etc.?

There are no easy answers to these questions. The comments and observations in this chapter are attempts to share some of the issues with others, and to make a few points which might be helpful to those whose experience of working with non-English families is minimal. They are based on several years of experience with West Indian and especially Asian children and families, and on the viewpoints of others with similar experiences.

The children

Children of all nations have developmental difficulties, ranging from a severe and fundamental handicap to less severe but often complex patterns of learning and behaviour. Equally, children of all nations appear to pass through similar developmental stages from birth to adolescence, although there are some variations between one culture and another (Bruner, 1974; Modgil and Modgil, 1980). It is worth remembering that cross-cultural developmental studies usually compare children living in their own non-western countries with children living in the west. Most of the children of non-English background referred to psychologists in England have had a considerable experience of English schooling and an English peer group, which has influenced their development considerably – possibly as much as, or even more than, their parents have in some ways. Thus, they may be assumed to be more like English children than they would be if they had not left their countries of origin. Indeed, regular contact with Asian and West Indian children makes one realize very quickly how similar they are to English children, though with certain interesting and often pleasing differences.

In the past there has often been criticism of the use of English or American standardized tests on children of West Indian or Asian background and culture. There is some justification for this, since many of the tests contain a large number of verbal items, or items which are based on a knowledge of English society and customs. However, it is suggested that a child who has had three to four years of English schooling, during which children of the same background have made good progress while he has experienced great difficulties, can be properly tested in a standardized intelligence test. The psychologist will, of course, always use great caution when interpreting the results of such tests with children of non-English background. If a child has *not* had the experience of English schooling, he needs to be given the experience with the additional help of an experienced ESL teacher before any attempt is made to understand the nature, and resolution of his difficulties (Desforges, 1982).

With younger children (the 3–5 year age range) the task may be in one way easier, and in another more difficult. Most standardized tests for pre-school children contain many non-verbal items. During an informal session with an non-English child, the psychologist who is familiar with the age group (and this is probably of crucial importance) can often obtain a good idea of the child's appropriate level of ability. In other words, a generally retarded Asian or West Indian child can be identified without too much difficulty by a psychologist who is familiar with the age group and the appropriate test material. On the other hand, there are occasions when this may be difficult with young children. This is true of English young children as well, of course, but the additional factor of a non-English speaking background, and perhaps lack of exposure to English objects, or even toys, indicates a need for caution. If a clear picture of a young child cannot be obtained during, say, two assessment sessions, a period of continuous assessment in a diagnostic unit is recommended so that the child's behaviour and performance can be monitored over a period of time.

Parents and psychologists

West Indian and Asian parents vary greatly in their ability to speak English, the degree to which they have become anglicized, and in the importance they attach to their own cultural or religious influences and creeds. In my own experience, it is rare for *both* parents to be completely lacking in English. West Indian families have English as their first language – though occasionally accent, or patois, can come between the individual and the psychologist. Asian families more usually use their mother-language at home, though it is rare, in my experience, to find that *neither* parent speaks at least some English. (It is usually the father, who has regular contact with English people at his work, who speaks English, but this is not invariably so. I have met parents where the mother's grasp of English, and her educational experience, are superior to her husband's.)

If the parents speak no English, an interpreter is essential. However, when at least one parent speaks some English, the value of using an interpreter might be outweighed by other factors. For example, one can never be sure how one's words, or the words of the parents, are actually being translated, or whether certain important nuances are lost. In my experience, it is nearly always possible to have a *fact-sharing* conversation with the parents of non-English children, even if it is impossible in some cases to do more than that. Thus, one can gather important information about the child's early life (birth and perinatal details, whether he walked and talked at the usual ages, how he behaves at home compared with his siblings, etc.), and also about the family (are they employed, is the housing adequate, do grandparents live with them?). Some psychologists might question the possibility – or the wisdom – of asking parents about their own background – thinking, perhaps, that these questions might emphasize their difference from the psychologist. However, I have found that nearly all such families are happy to talk about their own background, their families back home, their educational experience and so on, if one shows them genuine and sympathetic interest.

It is less easy to communicate to parents who have only a very basic understanding of English *why* one is concerned about their child and what one proposes to *do* about helping the child (and why). This is largely a language difficulty, but it also seems to be due to a culture gap. How, for example does an Asian family with little education and poor English perceive a white psychologist: as a figure of authority who must be obeyed else there might be trouble; or as someone who cannot possibly begin to understand *their* point of view, and must therefore be placated, or deflected from the task in hand?

These factors are particularly important when it is a question of communicating to parents that a child has a fundamental difficulty (such as a severe, or fairly severe, mental handicap) which may necessitate a special education placement. It is particularly important that they understand that the psychologist's comments are recommendations rather than directions to the parents. It is my experience that it can be extremely difficult to convey to parents with little English (or to *feel* that one has conveyed to them) that one wants to weigh up *with them* the advantages and disadvantages of moving their child from one school to another – either because the parents see the psychologist as an authority figure, or (perhaps) because they see her as having all the answers to the child's problems! It may, therefore, be necessary to engage the services of an interpreter – at least briefly – so that the parents' rights are explained to them clearly. (This is even more important with the advent of the 1981 Education Act, though it needs to be remembered that psychologists have always wanted to make recognition of, and allowance for, parents' wishes.)

Where the parents speak competent English, the fact-sharing is obviously much easier. There remains, nevertheless, a culture gap between parents and psychologist which can cause difficulties to a greater or lesser extent. Some non-English parents are very anglicized; others have not changed their perceptions or their attitudes greatly (if at all) since arriving in England. The psychologist is unlikely, without many years of experience of the different sub-groups within the main group (e.g. Asian subgroups of Muslim, Hindu, etc.) to know much about these perceptions and attitudes. She can, however, make certain assumptions in her contact with parents based on her knowledge of families, and of what it means to be a parent – for example, that the parents are acutely disappointed at the child's failure. Such disappointment, or sadness, is a normal response of all parents (though it may not necessarily be expressed openly and directly to the psychologist, or others), but it could well be even greater for those who have made a break with their past and come to England to give their children a good education and career. The psychologist may also be aware that certain cultural factors may be increasing the parental suffering. For example, she may know that in certain societies the first-born son is all-important to the father and that a defect in this child is particularly hard for the parents to bear. She may also suspect that, in some cases, the father might blame the mother for the child's problems or handicap. However, I have heard more than one Asian father say very emphatically of his wife: 'It is not her fault' – protecting her, perhaps, in his own mind from the criticism, real or imagined, of relatives.

A female psychologist may be able to establish a rapport with the child's mother even if the mother does not speak very good English, on the basis of a shared female identity. Many – even most – women of all societies know the joys, sorrows and conflicts of rearing children, and the difficulties associated with the domestic and maternal roles, particularly when the woman is also working outside the home. It is possible to use these shared factors as the basis for family therapy (see Campion, 1982) in many cases. The psychologist does, however, need to guard against the possibility of identifying too strongly with the child's mother. It is possible, for example, to feel indignant at the apparently unsupported state of the single West Indian woman with children, and to forget that she accepts this and has her own support networks. Equally (or perhaps even more likely) the psychologist may find herself over-concerned by the naturally quiet, passive acceptance of an Asian mother. It is too easy to interpret this in terms of depression or unhappiness. It may be, of course, but it is by no means necessarily so.

The child and the family system

Patterns of child rearing differ from country to country and from culture to culture as anyone who has spent time living with, or even observing, families in another country (even in Europe) are aware. Commenting on the differences is, however, a delicate matter, since one can so easily be influenced by the stereotypes associated with the country. Perhaps it is only reasonable to make comments when one has had a fairly broad experience of observing, and talking to, the children of another culture, and their families so that it becomes possible to notice how they usually behave. One's personal observations can then be linked with (or even contrasted with) the observations of others with similar experience.

Asian families seem more 'close' and mutually dependent/self-sufficient than English families. Divorce or separation is uncommon. The children are more docile and compliant than English children, and are taught to respect their parents in a father formal way that is uncommon in English or West Indian families. The father is the head of the household in all senses – though the way he undertakes this role depends on his own personality. Some Asian fathers mix authority with affection and some degree of flexibility; others are rigid, even punitive. The women nearly always accept their husband's role as head of the home, finding their *raison d'être* in being relatively subservient to him (de Lobo, 1978).

Asian parents appear to encourage hard work and high standards in their children. This has excellent results when the child has the potential to perform to a high level, but is (or can be) counter-productive, or even damaging when the child has little basic ability. Some of the Asian children I have seen have been children of relatively low ability made anxious by the over-expectation of their parents. Sometimes, however, such referrals can be quite rewarding. Parents will often respect one's suggestions that they should not expect too much of their child, who does not have quite the ability they hoped for.

West Indian children, on the other hand, are frequently brought up by their mothers alone. The fathers are more or less shadowy figures, who appear from time to time and offer some financial support, but who are rarely living permanently with the mother and children. The West Indian mothers seem to keep in touch with their mothers and sisters. They usually speak good English and are ready to communicate their anxieties about their children. By western standards, they seem a little over-strict at times, and it is not uncommon to come across families where religious beliefs are leading to rather extreme attitudes in the parents. The children themselves tend to be livelier and more extraverted than their English or Asian peers, although this is by no means always true (see de Lobo, 1978).

As far as the family system is concerned, there may be some risk in applying certain systems theories to non-English families. Lau (1984) comments: 'We handle phenomena from other cultures, using concepts and ideas derived from our own culture, and our feeling reactions derive from *this* culture matrix [but] . . . what happens when the rules, and the shared assumptions, are different?' She then draws attention to the Chinese tradition of supporting elderly relatives, even at the cost of the younger members of the family, and of placing fraternal loyalties above conjugal loyalty – traditions that are alien to English people.

Littlewood and Lipsedge (1982) make the point that psychiatric disturbance is expressed differently in different cultures. Thus, although the message of all cultures is 'don't be deviant', if a person *is* deviant his 'symptoms' tend to reflect certain cultural factors. A West Indian patient who is suffering from depression following the death of a relative may start talking about seeing ghosts. If he/she is suffering from some degree of paranoia, he/she may speak of being the subject of witchcraft. Thus, the patient uses the language and the beliefs of his cultural background as a method of communicating his feelings of distress to others.

Although these viewpoints need to be taken into consideration by those who work regularly with families from backgrounds which are different from that of the psychologist, I would like to suggest that there are many more similarities between the referred children from non-English backgrounds and their English peers than there are differences. Also, that the psychologist who is familiar with working with families, and is not too concerned by occasional confusion and misunderstandings, will probably be able to see certain family patterns repeating themselves in non-English families which are remarkably similar to those seen in referred English families.

Children of all countries need the mixture of affection, stability, discipline and clarity of communication from their parents which were mentioned in previous chapters. They also need parents who are reasonably in harmony with each other, and not too burdened by shadows from the past. It is quite often possible to be aware that things are not as they should be. It may be that the parents are trying to work too hard to make their way in a new country, and that they expect too much of their children both academically and in terms of emotional support for themselves. There may be difficulties in family relationships, hinted at perhaps during an interview, though not spoken about directly because of the need for family solidarity. At times, the discipline may appear too harsh.

Faced with the possibility that the referred child's symptoms reflect inadequacies – from the child's point of view – in the family system, the psychologist needs to decide what, if anything, she should do about it. She needs to decide if the family could make use of family sessions to help the referred child, or whether some other (and if so, what) method of help should be initiated.

The three cases of non-English referred children that follow illustrate briefly the factors involved.

Two young West Indian children

Both were referred with behaviour problems and learning difficulties. They were living with their mother, a single parent who, though able to care for the children well in a practical sense, had a very depressed and withdrawn personality. It was felt that the children's difficulties arose at least partly from a lack of stimulating interaction between the children and their mother, but family sessions seemed inappropriate since the mother was so unresponsive and her English difficult to understand. The children were offered special help within the education system, and the mother the support of a mother's group.

A girl from a Hindu family

K was referred aged 8 with confused, attention-seeking behaviour and very poor progress in school. Before seeing K, the psychologist spoke to the mother who brought her youngest child (a boy aged 2½ years) to the school for an interview with the head teacher and the psychologist. The mother struck the psychologist as a sad person with few inner resources. The psychologist was also disconcerted by the way the boy clung to his mother in a desperate way throughout the longish interview, ignoring a range of toys on a low table next to him. Most significant of all, however, was the change in the child when K joined the session. He ran to her, grabbing some of the toys, and asked her to play with him. She put him on her lap and played with him.

A further investigation revealed a very depressed and inadequate family, and that K was required to do most of the domestic tasks and look after her brother. Help for K was offered through the school (with remedial help in a small group). The help of social services was enlisted, and the younger child was given a place in a local social services day nursery.

A Sikh boy

He was referred aged 15 for stealing. The family had been in England for several years, and the father, a successful businessman, was greatly upset by his son's behaviour. The mother was very attached to the boy – their only child – and somewhat dependent on him to meet her emotional needs.

It was apparent that S – like many English children – was playing off one adult against the other over questions of discipline, pocket money, etc. Also, that the parents were finding it hard to accept that he was growing up and needed more independence. Sessions could be and were conducted with his family 'as if' they were English, though the mother's English was poor.

It is hoped that these brief case-histories indicate in some measure that the psychologist can use her understanding of family processes as part of the diagnostic task even if she is unfamiliar with the culture of the family she sees and at times work with families 'as if' they were of the same cultural background as herself.

Most important of all, in my view, is the need for the psychologist to guard against her own prejudices when seeing the families of children from other countries. She is unlikely to be concerned about the colour of her clients' skin, but she may find herself disconcerted by certain attitudes and ways of behaving which the family take for granted. This is probably most likely to arise in connection with the relationship between the child's parents, which might seem unusual or even offensive to the psychologist accustomed to English parents only. Asian women, for example, do seem very subservient to their husbands by English standards. They may not answer questions if their husband is present, even if they speak English, and the psychologist may need to insist politely that she wants to hear what the mother thinks. The psychologist may even be aware that an Asian girl is being prevented from following higher educational studies, or is being considered for an arranged marriage. Again, she needs to be able to accept and respect cultural traditions that are different from her own. It helps to remember the large number of English children who are experiencing stress as a result of *our* cultural practices (e.g. relatively easy divorce, lack of parental control during the adolescent period leading to drug-taking or delinquency).

17

The interrelationship between helping professionals

Children known to educational psychologists are not infrequently known to other professionals as well – in addition, that is, to their class teachers. Thus, a child might be attending a child guidance clinic or the child psychiatric department of a local hospital, while being helped at school by teachers who are following the recommendations of an educational psychologist. Or, the psychologist herself might be helping the child in counselling, play therapy or family therapy, whilst the family is also receiving help from the social services department. If the child has a physical problem, there may well be several doctors involved with the case as well as other professionals (speech therapists, physiotherapists, etc.). Sometimes these people are part of the same team (e.g. the child guidance team), and are therefore well known to each other. At other times they do not know each other well, but are occasionally drawn together to co-operate over a case, as is the situation from time to time with educational psychologists and social workers from the social services team. Sometimes they may be completely unknown to each other, as, for example, in the case of a hospital consultant who makes a recommendation on behalf of a child known to others working with that child and the family in the local authority.

Group and family processes

Psychologists have long had an interest in certain group processes, and in the way in which individuals co-operate (or fail to co-operate) with each other when required to undertake a particular task (see Brown, 1965). Recently, there has been an increased interest in the subject among many people with some of the impetus coming from the group-analytical movement (see Bion, 1961) and some from the family therapy movement. Both these schools of thought contribute to our understanding of the processes which prevail when a number of different people are required to co-operate with each other, though it is impossible to consider all of the theories and all of the factors. This chapter is an attempt to look briefly at *some* of the issues which might affect the educational psychologist and the referred child, with particular reference to family-systems theory.

The child guidance clinic and the school psychological service

Traditionally, the links between the child guidance team and the school psychological service have been close. The children seen by educational psychologists are often known to one or more members of the child guidance team (for example, psychiatrist(s), social worker(s) or psychotherapist(s)). In some areas, the two services work as a united team, with referrals being allocated to the professional who seems to have most to offer the particular child. In other cases, the relationship is more distant, and the teams function separately, referring children to each other as and when it seems necessary. In some (fortunately very few) cases, the relationship between the two teams is fraught with difficulties and antagonism. Some of the reasons can be found in a consideration of the family-type processes which prevail when any groups of individuals are regularly in close contact with each other.

Where the relationship between the child guidance team and the school psychological service has been good for a number of years, it is usually because the system has characteristics in common with a 'good enough' family system. That is to say, members are able to:

(a) respect the hierarchies in the system
(b) respect each other's boundaries (whilst accepting and acknowledging their own boundaries)
(c) communicate with others – disagreeing perhaps sometimes, but not to the point of taking up rigid, inflexible attitudes
(d) negotiate areas of difference and reconcile conflicting needs and viewpoints
(e) come to terms with certain inescapable and painful facts – primarily, perhaps, the difficulty or impossibility of changing the circumstances of some children's lives.

Senior members should, like parents, be able to make certain rules and take certain decisions without worrying too much about their own personal popularity. At the same time, they need to be able to recognize the viewpoints of less senior members, and that those people need the opportunity to grow and develop talents and skills which might well be different from their own. Free and open communication between individual members of the team should be possible, and there should be sufficient flexibility in the system for personal growth, development and change. However, the system itself needs to be stable enough not to be unduly upset or unbalanced by change in an individual member.

Where it has not been possible to achieve this flexible and yet stable system there may be difficulties expressed in dissenting voices and conflicting attitudes between members. In extreme cases, a total split may occur. (The division which has taken place between the school psychological service and the child guidance team in many areas reflects some of these personal 'family' difficulties. It also reflects other factors, outlined in the next section).

Wider networks

Educational psychologists are required to co-operate with a very large number of professionals not only in schools and in the two teams described above, but in other networks and systems (social services, hospital departments, etc.). Co-operation with this wider group is not the same as working with a familiar 'family'-type group, although there are some similarities. In some ways it is more difficult to work with people outside the familiar team since there are more unknown factors to contend with. In other ways it can be easier. For example, feelings of animosity are usually easier to bear when they arise as the result of communications with outsiders than if they arise within the 'family' group. On the other hand, disagreements with outsiders tend to be more difficult to resolve, and may result in entrenched attitudes which can be detrimental to the resolution of a particular problem. They may also result in people making recommendations or taking courses of action which are directly opposed to each other, with resulting confusion and anger in both professionals and parents alike.

One of the most important differences between co-operation in a family group and co-operation in a wider group is that the hierarchies of the system are less apparent, or even non-existent. Communications tend to founder because people are not sure what to expect of each other, or of who is in charge of what in a particular case. All members of the wider group are equals in the sense that each makes a uniquely valuable contribution to the discussion. On the other hand, their understanding and appreciation of the contributions of other members of the group may be very limited. There may be a tendency to undervalue other people's contributions or, at the other extreme, to overestimate the value of the contribution and the power of the person who makes it.

Nevertheless, though there may be little understanding between different professionals who are required to co-operate with each other over a particular case at times, and little structure to the group, certain family-system theories still apply. People still need to be able to respect each others boundaries and be aware of their own, to communicate with each other and negotiate areas of difficulty, and to come to terms with the limitations (their own and other peoples') to change the circumstances of some children's lives. And, as in families, certain negative and destructive systems can arise – a collusive 'sub-system' perhaps, which undermines the activities and recommendations of others.

Sticking points between professionals

There are various difficulties which can arise when the educational psychologist is a member of a group of professionals who are helping a referred child, whether or not the group is a close-knit one. It is suggested that possible sticking points can be usefully considered separately:

(1) different professional *viewpoints* arising from different training (e.g. in medicine, psychology, social work, speech therapy)
(2) different professional *responsibility* and authority (e.g. to diagnose, to recommend a change of school, to take into care, to recommend and carry out a course of treatment)
(3) parental perception of the various roles, powers, functions, etc. of the various professionals
(4) lack of communication between the various professionals
(5) hidden conflict, expressed indirectly, between the different professionals.

Differing professional viewpoints

Perhaps the most potentially problematic areas from the point of view of the psychologist, lie in the different viewpoints between psychologists and psychiatrists, psychologists and other doctors (mainly paediatricians), and psychologists and social workers.

Psychologists and psychiatrists Psychologists and psychiatrists are frequently involved with the same children (either in the child guidance team, or where there is a flourishing child psychiatric department in a local hospital) and over the years have had to establish a *modus vivendi*, in spite of various difficulties. Part of the problem lies in the theoretical models and training of the professionals, and part lies in the relative positions of power and responsibility (see next section). Psychologists and psychiatrists do not (on the whole) use the same terminology. A behavioural psychologist using the language and models of learning theory discussing a child with a psychiatrist who is analytically trained may appear to be talking completely at cross-purposes. This is not necessarily the case (although it occasionally is!) but the misunderstandings can result in much confusion – even anger. The same is true, of course, if the psychologist is speaking in family-systems terms, and the psychiatrist applying a within-child model of child disturbance. Most of the disagreements between psychologists and psychiatrists are resolved, or avoided, by each deciding not to encroach on the other's territory. However, they are sometimes of fundamental importance.

A child with communication difficulties was being treated with behavioural methods, and a computer-based learning programme, in a special unit for children with language difficulties. Dissatisfied with her progress, the parents consulted a psychiatrist, who diagnosed severe emotional and social difficulties, and recommended psychotherapy for the child. Considerable antagonism was aroused among the professionals previously concerned with the case when the psychiatrist's viewpoint was conveyed to them.

Psychologists and other members of the medical profession Doctors are trained to make a diagnosis according to the various medical categories of condition, while psychologists are concerned mainly with what children can and cannot do, and how they behave. This may be a stumbling-block in the case of a handicapped child, who might be described in different terms by a psychologist and a paediatrician. For example, a doctor puts a medical 'label' on the child (e.g. Down's syndrome), a label which, for the parents particularly, is of prime importance. A psychologist will be more concerned to discover what the child can and cannot do (some Down's children develop quite well and can manage in mainstream education, some cannot) and to offer the parents realistic and practical advice about their child's future and education.

A hospital consultant might recommend a course of treatment, unaware that other factors make the recommendation inappropriate. Or, he may make a particular recommendation in connection with the child's educational needs, without referring to the professionals in the area where the child lives and who may be in a better position to assess the child, and make a realistic recommendation to help him, based on what is actually available in the area. Two examples are given, to illustrate these points.

A child with a slight partial hearing loss was given a hearing aid in a large teaching hospital. The consultant was unaware that the child came from a family with multi-social and psychiatric problems, and that the mother was hoping to persuade the local authority that it was the child's hearing loss which created her (severe) behaviour problems, rather than accept the need for psychiatric/psychological intervention and, perhaps, special schooling. The consultant's contact with the mother and her prescription for a hearing aid for the child gave the mother the opportunity and the incentive to avoid visits to the psychologist and the psychiatrist, and to pressure the authority for help for her 'deaf' child. A visit to a partial-hearing unit was arranged and it was finally made apparent to the mother that her child's problems were in no way comparable to the difficulties of the other children in the unit who had severe speech and language problems, and no behavioural difficulties. Soon after, the child stopped wearing her hearing aid. After considerable negotiations involving many professionals, she was placed in a secondary school with a group of children with social and emotional difficulties.

A consultant recommended a boarding school to the parents of a 'disturbed' child, who asked the local authority for this, unaware that the recommendation needed to come from the psychologist or psychiatrist. The authority had stopped funding boarding school places except in extreme cases. The psychologist then had great difficulty working with the parents in family therapy, since they clung to the belief that a boarding school place would (and should) be available to them if they continued to press for it.

In both these cases, recommendations made by consultants based outside the local educational authority made difficulties for those working in the authority, who needed to be able to consider the child's needs and development as a whole, drawing on available provisions and resources to do so. It would, however, be unreasonable to suggest that it is only consultants and their recommendations that can create problems. There are times when psychologists might also be guilty of making decisions which undermine the work of others.

Psychologists and social workers Educational psychologists frequently need to co-operate with social workers – either those who are members of their own educational psychology/child guidance team, or those who are employed by social services. The nature of this co-operation varies greatly: it may, for example, be a 'therapeutic' co-operation, with the psychologist and the social worker taking a family in family therapy. Or, it may be a 'management' co-operation with the social worker supporting the family in a practical sense (e.g. helping with finance; supervising access to the children if the parents are separated), and the psychologist helping the teachers with the child at school. Or, it may be some other arrangement between the psychologist and the social worker designed to suit the individual case.

Psychologists are trained – on the whole – to see children as individuals, though they may later see the need to understand them as part of a system, or group. Social workers are – on the whole – trained with a much greater emphasis on, and awareness of, the needs and the pressures of society at large, although child guidance social workers are particularly skilled in working with the parents of referred children.

Each case is different though in all cases practical co-operation between educational psychologist and social worker is needed. This means that they need to decide on their respective roles and the goals they hope to achieve with a particular child and his family. It also means that they may have to come to terms with second-best (or even failure) in trying to help many muddled, deprived and disorganized families.

Professional responsibility and authority

The responsibilities, and the authority, of each of the professionals who might be involved with a particular child vary greatly. Consultants have the power to diagnose, and the status of their profession, but they do not have the authority to remove children from their parents as social workers do. Nor, of course, do educational psychologists, although *they* have the possibility of recommending special education – a recommendation which may occasionally conflict with the wishes of a child's social worker. It is not unknown, for example, for psychologists to suggest to a teacher that they think a particular child might need special education when a social worker has been working hard with parents to avoid this.

Similarly, it is not uncommon for educational psychologists

to be asked to advise a school about handling a child who is receiving treatment from a psychiatrist or a psychologist in a clinic or a hospital. Thus, responsibility is divided – the psychiatrist taking responsibility for the child's treatment, the psychologist for his behaviour at school. This method of working, though it can be valuable, is often particularly stressful for the psychologist. In her regular contact with the school, she may hear details of the child's behaviour which make her wonder about the effectiveness of the psychiatric treatment. Although she may offer suggestions to the class teachers on handling the child, or draw up a behaviour modification programme, she may also be somewhat resentful that the case is taking up so much of her time when it is 'really' someone else's (i.e. the psychiatrist's) responsibility. On the other hand, the psychologist, if she is honest with herself, may not necessarily prefer a situation where the psychiatrist visits the school and makes recommendations to teachers on behalf of the child which she does not necessarily agree with. Although disagreement about treatment methods may not matter very much in a particular case, it may matter in the long term if the psychiatrist visits a school regularly and always makes recommendations which differ from those made by the psychologist.

The psychologist herself may at times experience conflict about her responsibilities towards individuals. Where, for example, does her responsibility lie in cases where she is aware that a particular child is not getting what he needs from the education department – to the child, or to the department?

Parental perceptions

The psychologist can never be certain how the parents perceive her role. When she is working with a group, she can never be sure how the parents' perceptions of the *other people* colour their perceptions of her, and her role.

If the parents are very attached to one professional person –

perhaps the social worker – in the team, they may be disinclined to listen to the psychologist if her opinion is different from that of the social worker. On the other hand, parents may expect too much of the psychologist if they are disenchanted with more familiar professionals or disagree with what they are saying about the child.

Much depends on the nature and severity of the child's problems, and on the parents' own anxieties and needs. Where the problem is severe and largely intractable, parents may move from one professional adviser to another hoping that *someone* has an answer to the problem. They may distort the viewpoint of other people when talking to the psychologist. Psychologists occasionally find that the parents of a severely handicapped child say that the doctor has told them the child is 'all right'. The doctor may have misled the parents of course, but it is more likely that his comments have been misinterpreted since they are too painful to bear.

Communication between various professionals

Professionals who are involved with a child and his family usually wish to know if others are also involved, particularly if recommendations are likely to be made which might interfere with their own efforts to help the child. This may seem obvious, but it can be forgotten or ignored in the enthusiasm for a task in hand. Thus, a professional may make a quick recommendation based on his own perception of the child's problems, regardless of the nature of the interventions which the child and his family are already receiving, and the wishes of those already involved.

P, aged 9, was the subject of a care order, following physical abuse from his parents. The social worker consulted a child psychiatrist for a psychiatric report on the child to see if he could be regarded as suitable for a fostering placement. P was receiving help in a special unit for children with learning difficulties.

The psychiatrist called a case conference at short notice and the educational psychologist was unable to attend. Teachers attended, and described several things that P had done at school, which prompted the psychiatrist to suggest that special education was indicated. In fact, P had *improved* considerably at school, in spite of his occasional outbursts of difficult behaviour, and it seemed unlikely that better provision could be made for him in a special school.

Once special schooling was suggested, however, social workers and teachers seemed to think this would be the answer to his problems. Indeed, the suggestion seemed to divert attention from what was actually a much more serious situation for the child – the breakdown of relationships in his family, and the need for developing a new relationship with his foster parents. Pressure was put on the educational psychologist to comply with the wishes of the case conference.

In this situation, better communication between the professionals could have avoided the problem. The case conference could, for example, have been arranged at a time which was convenient to the educational psychologist as well as to others.

It is not always the psychologist who is the 'victim' however. *N's family* was being helped by a social worker who had spent much time and effort keeping the family together. She knew that the mother feared a change of schools for the child, and was disconcerted to find that the educational psychologist had suggested this possibility to the class teacher without discussing it openly with the parents first. The parents felt very let down, even when they were told that they didn't have to accept this recommendation. Indeed, they appeared to feel that there had been a collusion between the social worker and the psychologist to move their child to special education.

Hidden conflict expressed indirectly

Just as members of the same family may not necessarily express their disagreement (or conflict) openly, but dress it up in humorous remarks, or pretend it does not exist, professionals may be tempted to similar tactics. Individual professionals may seek to express their own fears of failure or incompetence (real or imagined), and their own annoyance with others (or with the situation as they see it), in many different and indirect ways. They may, for example, suggest that a particular child (or his family) are beyond help, or that the fault lies with other professionals or other groups, within society at large or with the politico-economic system. Although there is often some truth in these allegations, it is obviously unhelpful if people become negative, angry or defensive, simply because there is no ideal solution to the problem which they are required to tackle. Again, some flexibility and reality is needed. Thus, if certain provisions for children (e.g. residential boarding school provision) cease to exist, it should be possible for people to co-operate to produce substitute facilities and provisions – even if these are not felt to be as good as the original arrangements or provisions.

Sometimes the conflict, and the anger between professionals at their own helplessness or the perceived helplessness/incompetence of others, can result in action being taken which is not necessarily in the child's best interest. Thus a child may be moved because this is a *possible* solution, when the *impossible* (or more difficult) solutions have been attempted and have failed.

Sometimes, unfortunately, individual workers can become demoralized or defeated by the various difficulties (real or imagined) and by their own inability to cope with the situation. Help is then needed for that person, if he is not to feel that he carries the burden alone.

Disorganized families

Some families seen by educational psychologists will have had considerable experience of contact with many different professionals. Some will, unfortunately, have developed methods of avoiding facing up to certain realities by moving from one agency to another – from social services to child psychiatry to the school psychological services, and so on. Many of these families tend to be highly disorganized, and the contact between the different professionals who attempt to help them may reflect that lack of organization and confusion. Reder and Kraemer (1980) describe the way in which the helping professionals can be drawn into a disorganized family system. Communications break down between the professionals, people identify too strongly with individual members of the family, there appear to be no rules, no boundaries and no recognizable plan of action. Though Reder and Kraemer write from the viewpoint of the psychiatrist, their description of the situation will be both familiar and helpful to educational psychologists working in a local authority (see also Reder, 1983).

The individual *and* the system

We have seen in earlier chapters how individuals need to be able to adapt to changing circumstances, and to come to terms with certain painful realities of life. The same applies to professional people. In the nature of things, power tends to shift and change. Individuals who once reigned supreme and took decisions on their own may find themselves having to consult with or even defer to the wishes and viewpoint of others. Some welcome this change, others find it hard to accept. With the passage of time, some people may no longer feel themselves to be as competent, or as valued and respected, as they once were. They may be overlooked in the promotion race, and passed over by younger people. They may become ill, or burdened by domestic responsibilities. These and other factors put pressure on individuals. Ways in which the individuals cope, or try to come to terms with, their difficulties may place a strain on the system in which they work. Fears, anxieties, uncertainties will not necessarily be expressed directly – any more than feelings of resentment, jealousy or antagonism. They are, perhaps, more likely to be expressed indirectly. Thus, an individual who feels himself to be under pressure for reasons which lie within himself, or outside the setting of his work, may project his angry feelings on to colleagues. He may blame others unreasonably, or be resistant to their viewpoint. He may take up fixed attitudes towards others or avoid taking his share of responsibility. In extreme cases he may withdraw from contact with others altogether.

The difficult, unreasonable behaviour of one individual tends to set in motion (at least in some measure) difficult, unreasonable behaviour in other members of the team. This is particularly noticeable, of course, when the team is a close-knit one. Other people become hurt, angry, defensive and rigid, and the system, which might have been previously 'good enough', becomes confused, split or incapacitated. Collusive sub-systems may form. People may withdraw into themselves, or seek employment elsewhere.

There are also unseen and complex factors related to the fantasies which are part-and-parcel (to a greater or lesser extent) of human thinking – although we might wish it to be otherwise. For example, adults may carry with them feelings of 'infantile omnipotence' which belong to early childhood or perhaps feelings of paranoia which also belong to that time. Klein (1963) describes the way in which certain patterns of behaviour which develop during the first year of life relate to both the fantasies of the child and the realities of the outside world, and set the pattern of behaviour of the individual throughout his life. Her work is both important and undervalued as a description of the behaviour of both individuals and of systems.

18

Family-systems theory and the practising educational psychologist

Traditional theories of child psychology and psychiatry are based on the notion that there is 'something wrong with' the referred child which needs to be treated or remediated. These within-child models have been challenged in different ways by different people. In educational psychology the tendency has been to look increasingly at the school system and at the way in which the attitudes or actions of teachers might be creating or maintaining unsatisfactory behaviour in pupils. In child psychiatry (and increasingly in child psychology) the tendency is to focus on the child as part of his family system, and to concentrate on promoting change in that system for the benefit of the child. The common factor of these approaches is that their proponents have made a radical shift away from the idea that the presenting 'symptom' (whatever its nature) reflects a fundamental aspect of the child's own personality, towards the notion that the problem is a function of some *dys*function in the family or school system which includes the child.

During the course of this book, several children and their families have been described and discussed from a family-systems viewpoint. In helping the children, the psychologist chose to focus on their behaviour and their performance as a function of certain experiences within their family system – or at least to incorporate that understanding into a programme of help for the child. In some cases, work with the family continued over a period of months; in others, only one or two interviews took place – although even a single interview was regarded as valuable in that it allowed the psychologist to weigh up the various possibilities for helping the child, as well as helping her to diagnose the nature of his difficulties.

The child *and* the system

Although the emphasis has been on the child as part of his family system, I have tried not to lose sight of the child as an individual – or, indeed, of *people* as individuals. In Chapter 2 attention was paid to the various models of individual child development, all of which, in my view, contribute to our understanding of the behaviour of individuals and of systems. Some of the children were also discussed in terms of their individual psychological assessment – although this discussion was brief in view of the theme of the book. (The individual assessment of children has, in any case, been given extensive cover in other books, and my purpose was principally to indicate how it can be incorporated into work with the family.)

Educational psychologists need, for various reasons, to be able to take these different perspectives of referred children as and when it seems appropriate; and to be able to consider the child in terms of his own individual development and needs and or as an integral part of his family or school system. I am reminded of certain experiments and exercises in visual perception which form part of all degree courses in psychology. The viewer is involved in shifting his frame of reference as he looks at a picture from the figure to the background, and vice versa, or from one way of 'making sense of' a picture to another. Different figures seem to emerge to be replaced by others depending on the way in which the viewer focuses on the picture. It is perhaps not too fanciful to suggest that the educational psychologist seeing a referred child is in a similar position. She can choose to focus on the child himself, bringing his personality, viewpoint and needs to the foreground while (largely) disregarding the background; she can focus on the background which surrounds and includes the child; or she can focus on the whole picture and on the interrelationship between the various parts which make up the whole.

Although practising educational psychologists will develop their own preferred ways of working (which may be either primarily systems-based, or mainly child-centred), they need to be able to switch perspective according to the needs of the child(ren), the nature of the difficulties and the availability of resources. Those who have developed their skills and understanding of systems still need to hold on to their understanding of children as individuals. This understanding is of course necessary to fulfil the requirements of the 1981 Education Act which makes the individual psychological assessment of certain children mandatory. It is also necessary because it is fundamental to the practice of child psychology. In addition, an understanding of child psychology increases immeasurably the psychologist's ability to understand the 'child in the adult' and, therefore, the nature of adult systems too.

I would also suggest that attempts to focus on the family or school system to the exclusion – or partial exclusion – of an understanding of the individual can lead to a situation where people avoid facing up to the reality of the child's problem(s). A programme of help for the child, however undertaken, must include some recognition that the child 'has a problem' in the sense that he behaves in ways that he should not, seems unable to learn as others do, or has a physical defect. A tactful recognition in front of the child himself that there are difficulties is often a great relief to the child. It brings the problem into the open so that it may be seriously considered by others and, if possible, alleviated with the co-operation of the child himself. In some cases, particularly those involving a more serious and perhaps physical handicap or defect, the total progamme of help for the child may need to include a coming to terms with the child's handicap by all members of the family.

The 1981 Education Act

Some of the children described in this book fall into the category of children with special educational needs as defined in the 1981 Education Act; others do not. At the time of writing the Act is too recent to be able to make a clear distinction between those children who will and those who will not need Statements of Needs. Indeed, the way in which the Act is being implemented throughout the country is also unclear at present.

The methods of working which have been described fit comfortably with the requirements of the 1981 Act. They allow the psychologist to form a relationship with the child's parents at an early stage and, if it seems necessary, to discuss with them the provisions and the requirements of the Act.

The value of family-systems theory to the practising educational psychologist

I have attempted to demonstrate how family-systems theory can be used regularly by practising educational psychologists in their efforts to help referred children. The method described, which is illustrated by case-histories which will be familiar to all educational psychologists, is, I believe, useful for the following reasons.

(1) It acts as a starting-point for understanding some of the *fundamental* reasons for the child's failure.
(2) It allows the psychologist to make a positive and realistic relationship with the child's parents at an early stage and to offer them support and understanding as well as the child.
(3) It gives the psychologist an additional skill which she can use flexibly, and as a supplement to other methods of helping a child (e.g. school-based work).
(4) It fills a growing need for educational psychologists to

extend and develop their clinical skills as child psychologists.

These points bear further brief examination.

Understanding the reasons for a child's failure, or behavioural disturbance

A few years ago, child psychology was committed to behaviourism, which formed the bedrock of academic psychology and therefore of the training of psychologists. Little attempt was made to understand the reasons why people behave in the ways that they do. Today, although psychologists still use behaviour modification to good effect, many are also interested in techniques for helping people that are based on some degree of understanding: counselling, psychotherapy, group therapy, play therapy and family therapy. In other words, psychologists have recognized that it is often helpful to understand the way in which the *experience* of an individual (both in terms of past events, and in terms of present-day thoughts and feelings) may have created difficulties for him.

It is my belief that many children fail in school, and show signs of behavioural disturbance, for reasons which are closely related to difficulties within the family. The difficulties are not necessarily easy to see or to understand. They may be related to past traumatic events, to present-day anxieties, to relatively unsatisfactory parental attitudes, as well as to the more generally understood and accepted social problems (e.g. lack of money, ill-health, poor housing). The psychologist who understands the relationship between the child's experience at home and his difficulties at school, and can use this knowledge in a positive manner, is probably more likely to be able to help the child.

A link with the child's parents

Where children are referred to an educational psychologist, parents are almost always involved from the beginning. Their commitment to the idea of referral may or may not be great. At times, pressure may have been brought to bear on them to persuade them to agree to the referral.

In all cases, it is helpful if the psychologist can form a relationship with the child's parents as soon as possible after the referral is made. This relationship, however, is likely to be most effective if the psychologist manages to keep sufficient space between herself and the parents to allow for a dispassionate (and non-judgemental) look at the family system.

I would stress, yet again, that the psychologist, in undertaking work based on family-systems theory, does not seek to blame or criticize the child's parents – they, too, are frequently victims of their own past experience, of present-day hardship or confusion, and sometimes of their own children's behaviour. Virtually all parents want to do the best for their children, and have the ability to make use of the support offered to them by the psychologist, to the ultimate benefit of their children.

An additional tool for the psychologist

There is (nearly) always more than one way of helping a referred child. Sometimes it is more feasible and more practical to focus on the child in the school setting; at other times, it is better to concentrate on helping him outside the school. There are usually a range of options available to the psychologist, and it is a question of selecting the one which is likely to be helpful and possible to implement.

Although not all psychologists will wish to develop their methods of working along the lines described in this book, all can benefit from an understanding of family processes and family-systems theory. It is possible even in one family interview to obtain information which is diagnostically useful. In addition to this, however, an understanding of family processes increases the psychologist's ability to understand *all* social systems and groups (e.g. schools) and the relationship between different groups (e.g. schools, social services, the child guidance clinic).

The developing role of the educational psychologist

During the 1970s the discipline of educational psychology underwent a considerable change. Psychologists began to develop confidence in themselves, and in their ability to work on their own rather than remain exclusively a part of a child guidance team. They also became aware of the fact that certain school-based interventions were extremely effective in helping troubled children, and children who were failing in the school system. Thus the extent and the range of their work increased considerably.

It seems likely that the 1980s and 1990s will bring further changes to the practice of educational psychology, for several reasons. First, the 1981 Education Act makes it a statutory requirement for certain children to see an educational psychologist. Although this cannot be regarded entirely as an unmixed blessing (for example, it may well increase the amount of paperwork for psychologists, and others, without necessarily improving provisions for children) it should eventually result in an increase in the number of psychologists and in a general increase in their skills and expertise.

Secondly (and related to the first reason), there is the natural tendency for all professions (particularly young professions) to seek to develop from relatively narrow beginnings to wider fields of competence and expertise. Thirdly, there is the undeniable (and depressing) fact of the increase in troubled, disturbed, even violent behaviour in the young, which suggests a growing need for educational psychologists to develop to a greater extent their skills as therapists of groups, families and individuals, in addition to their skills of assessment and classroom intervention. This represents a considerable challenge to educational psychologists who are already burdened with work which they often have little time to complete as thoroughly as they would like. In addition, the shift involved in moving from the task of observation, measurement and instruction to one of therapy can bring with it special problems. It is, unfortunately, a good deal easier and less stressful to deal in the facts and figures of a child's performance, than to involve oneself in the often painful events of his life, and of the lives of other members of his family. Presumably, psychologists who wish to undertake this type of work regularly will look for further training, and perhaps join a support group or ask for supervision of cases.

I would not however wish to end on such a cautious, even pessimistic note. Rather, I would like to suggest that the psychologist who works regularly with families in an attempt to help children overcome behavioural difficulties and learning problems not only increases her effectiveness but adds immeasurably to her understanding of the complexity and richness of human behaviour.

References

Ackerman, N. W. (1958) *The Psychodynamics of Everyday Life*, New York and London, Basic Books.

Ackerman, N. W. (1966) *Treating the Troubled Family*, New York and London, Basic Books.

Aponte, H. J. (1976) 'The family-school interview: an eco-structural approach', *Family Processes*, 15, 303–13.

Bandura, A. (1971) 'Psychotherapy based upon modelling principles', in Bergin, A. E. and Garfield, S. L. (eds) *Handbook of Psychotherapy and Behaviour Change*, New York, Wiley.

Bateson, G., Jackson, D. D., Haley, J. and Weakland, J. H. (1956) 'Towards a theory of schizophrenia', *Behavioural Science* 1(4), 251–64.

Bentovim, A. (1979) 'Towards creating a focal hypothesis for brief focal family therapy', *Journal of Family Therapy*, 1, 125–36.

Bentovim, A. and Kinston, W. (1978) 'Brief focal family therapy when the child is the referred patient. 1. Clinical', *Journal of Child Psychology and Psychiatry*, 19, 1–12.

Bion, W. (1961) *Experience in Groups*, London, Tavistock.

Bowlby, J. (1979) *The Making and Breaking of Affectional Bonds*, London, Tavistock.

Bromwich, R. (1981) *Working with Parents and Infants. An Interactional Approach*, Baltimore, University Park Press.

Brown, R. (1965) *Social Psychology*, London, Collier-Macmillan.

Bruner, J. S. (1974) *Relevance of Education*, Harmondsworth, Penguin.

Bugental, D. E., Love, L. R., Kaswan, J. W. and April, C. (1971) 'Verbal – non-verbal conflicts in parental messages to normal and disturbed children', *Journal of Abnormal Psychology*, 77(1), 6–10.

Burton, A., Miller, A. and Willis, B. (1981) 'A workshop for parents of pre-school children with delayed development', *Journal of the Association of Educational Psychologists*, 5(5).

Burton-White, B. L. (1975) 'Critical influences and the origin of competence', *Merrill-Palmer Quarterly*, 21, 243–66.

Bushell, R., Miller, A. and Robson, D. (1982) 'Parents as remedial teachers: an account of a paired-reading project with junior school failing readers and their parents', *Journal of the Association of Educational Psychologists*, 5(9).

Cameron, R. J. (ed.) (1982) *Working Together: Portage in the UK*, Windsor, National Foundation for Educational Research/ Nelson.

Campbell, D., Reder, P., Draper, R. and Pollard, D. (1983) *Working with the Milan Method: Twenty Questions*, London, Institute of Family Therapy.

Campion, J. (1982) 'Young Asian children with learning and behaviour problems: a family therapy approach', *Journal of Family Therapy*, 4(2).

Campion, J. (1984) 'Psychological services for children: using family therapy in the setting of a school psychological service', *Journal of Family Therapy*, 6(1).

Carter, B. and McGoldrick, M. (eds) (1980) *The Family Life-cycle: A Framework for Family Therapy*, New York, Gardner Press.

Caspari, I. (1974) in Varma, V. (ed.) *Psychotherapy Today*, London, Constable.

Chazan, M. (1982) 'Disadvantage, behaviour problems and reading difficulties', *Journal of the Association of Educational Psychologists*, 5(10).

Coghill, S., Alexandra, H., Caplan, H., Robson, K., Kumar, R.

Impact of Maternal Depression in the First Year of Life on a Child's Subsequent Cognitive Development. Joint project, University College Hospital and the Institute of Psychiatry (submitted for publication).

Dare, C. and Pincus, L. (1978) *Secrets in the Family*, London and Boston, Faber & Faber.

De'Ath, E. (1982) 'Interventions with families: preparing the way for teaching parenting skills', *Journal of Family Therapy*, 4(3), 229–44.

De Lobo, E. (1978) *Children of Immigrants to Britain*, London, Hodder & Stoughton.

Desforges, M. (1978) 'Assessment of bi-cultural, bi-lingual children,' *Journal of the Association of Educational Psychologists*, 5(10).

Doane, J. A. (1978) 'Family interaction and communication deviance in disturbed and normal families. A review of research', *Family Processes*, 17.

Dollard, J. and Miller, N. (1950) *Personality and Psychotherapy*, New York, McGraw-Hill.

Douglas, J. (1981) 'Behavioural family therapy and the influence of a systems framework', *Journal of Family Therapy*, 3(4), 327–38.

Featherstone, H. (1981) *A Difference in the Family*, New York, Basic Books.

French, A. P. (1977) *Disturbed Children and their Families*, New York, Human Sciences Press.

Freud, A. (1967) *The Ego and the Mechanisms of Defense* (1937), New York, International Press.

Freud, A. (1981) *Psycho-analytic Psychology of Normal Development*, London, Hogarth Press.

Freud, S. (1963–74) 'The ego and the id' (1923) in *The Complete Psychological Works of Sigmund Freud*, London, Hogarth Press.

Gillham, W. E. C. (ed.) (1978) *Reconstructing Educational Psychology*, London, Croom Helm.

Gregory, S. *Advising Parents of Deaf Children – Is Psychology Relevant?*, Paper given at the conference of the developmental section of the British Psychological Society, Durham University, September 1982.

Gurman, A. (1981) *Handbook of Family Therapy*, New York, Brunner/Mazel.

Haldane, D. and McCluskey, U. (1982) 'Existentialism and family therapy: a neglected perspective', *Journal of Family Therapy*, 4(2).

Haley, J. (1978) *Problem-solving Therapy*, London, Harper & Row.

Herbert, M. (1981) *Behavioural Treatment of Problem Children: A Practice Manual*, London, Academic Press.

Hurford, H. (1983) 'School and family guidance: a communication systems approach to casework', *Association of Educational Psychologists Journal*, 6(2).

Jenkins, H. (1981) '"Can I (let you let me) leave?" Therapy with the adolescent and his family', *Journal of Family Therapy*, Vol. 3, no. 2.

Kinston, W. and Bentovim, A. (1978) 'Brief focal family therapy when the child is the referred patient: 2. Methodology and results', *Journal of Child Psychology and Psychiatry*, 19, 119–43.

Klein, M. (1932) *The Psycho-analysis of Children*, London, Hogarth Press.

Klein, M. (1963) 'Our adult world and its roots in infancy', in Klein, M. (ed.) *Our Adult World*, London, Heinemann.

Kolvin, I., Garside, R. F., Nicol, A. R., Macmillan, A., Wolstenholme, F. and Leitch, I. M. (1981) *Help Starts Here. The Maladjusted Child in the Ordinary School*, London, Tavistock.

Laing, R. D. and Esterson, A. (1970) *Sanity, Madness and the Family*, Harmondsworth, Penguin.

Lau, A. (1984) 'Transcultural issues in family therapy', *Journal of Family Therapy*, 6(2).

Lidz, T. (1984) 'A developmental theory', in Shershow, J. C. (ed.) *Schizophrenia, Science and Practice*, Cambridge, Mass., Harvard University Press, 69–95.

Lieberman, S. (1980) *Transgenerational Family Therapy*, London, Croom Helm.

Littlewood, R. and Lipsedge, M. (1982) *Aliens and Alienists*, Harmondsworth, Penguin.

Luterman, D. (1979) *Counselling Parents of Hearing-impaired Children*, Boston, Mass., Little, Brown.

McMichael, P. (1979) 'The hen or the egg?' Which comes first – anti-social emotional disorder or reading disability?', *British Journal of Educational Psychology*, 49, part 3.

Marmor, J. and Woods, S. M. (1980) *The Interface between the Psychodynamic and Behavioural Therapies*, London and New York, Plenum Medical Books.

Meichenbaum, D. (1977) *Cognitive-Behaviour Modification: An Interpretive Approach*, London and New York, Plenum Press.

Minuchin, S. (1974) *Families and Family Therapy*, London, Tavistock.

Minuchin, S. and Fishman, H. C. (1981) *Family Therapy Techniques*, Cambridge, Mass. and London, Harvard University Press.

Mittler, P. and Mittler, H. (1983) *Developing Horizons in Special Education* 2, Stratford-upon-Avon, National Council for Special Education.

Modgil, S. and Modgil, C. (1980) *Towards a Theory of Psychological Development*, Windsor, National Foundation for Educational Research.

Moore, S., Nicolski, I. and Presland, J. (1981) 'A workshop for parents of young handicapped children', *Journal of the Association of Educational Psychologists*, 5(5).

Morgan, R. and Lyon, E. (1979) 'Paired-reading – a preliminary report on a technique for parental tuition of reading-retarded children', *Journal of Child Psychology and Psychiatry*, 20, 151–9.

Murgatroyd, S. (ed.) (1980) *Helping the Troubled Child*, London, Harper & Row.

Noonan, E. (1984) *Counselling Young People*, London, Methuen.

Palazzoli, M. S., Boscolo, L., Cechin, G. and Prata, G. (1978) *Paradox and Counter-paradox*, New York, Jason Aronson.

Pilling, D. and Kellmer-Pringle, M. (1978) *Controversial Issues in*

Child Development, London, Paul Elek for National Children's Bureau.

Presland, J. L. (1974) 'Modifying behaviour now', *Special Education Forward Trends*, 1(3), 20–2.

Presland, J. L. (1980) 'Behaviour modification and secondary schools', in Upton, G. and Gobell, A. (eds) *Behaviour Problems in the Comprehensive School*, Faculty of Education, University College, Cardiff.

Pugh, Gillian (1982) *Parents as Partners. Intervention Schemes and Group Work with Parents of Handicapped Children*, London, National Children's Bureau.

Ravenette, A. T. (1979) 'Specific reading difficulties, appearance and reality', *Journal of the Association of Educational Psychologists*, 4(10).

Reder, P. (1983) 'Disorganized families and the helping professions: "Who's in Charge of What?"', *Journal of Family Therapy*, 5(1).

Reder, P. and Kraemer, S. (1980) 'Dynamic aspects of professional collaboration in child guidance referral', *Journal of Adolescence*, 3, 165–73.

Richman, N., Stevenson, J. and Graham, P. J. (1982) 'Pre-school to school: behavioural study', in Schaffer, R. (ed.) *Behavioural Development: A Series of Monographs*, London, Academic Press.

Roe, M. (1978) 'Medical and psychological concepts of problem behaviour', in Gillham, W. E. C. (ed.) *Reconstructing Educational Psychology*, London, Croom Helm.

Rubinstein, B. and Levitt, N. (1977) 'Learning difficulties related to a special form of mothering', *International Journal of Psychoanalysis*, 58, 45–55.

Sarason, I. G. (1978) 'A cognitive social learning approach to juvenile delinquency', in Hare, R. D. and Schelling, D. (eds) *Psychopathic Behavior: Approaches to Research*, New York, Wiley.

Satir, V. (1967) *Conjoint Family Therapy*, Palo Alto, Calif., Science and Behavior Books.

Schaffer, H. R. (1977) *Studies in Mother-Infant Interaction*, London, Academic Press.

Scharff, D. E. (1982) *The Sexual Relationship. An Object–Relations View of Sex and the Family*, London, Routledge & Kegan Paul.

Skynner, A. C. R. (1976a) *One Flesh: Separate Persons*, London, Constable.

Skynner, A. C. R. (1976b) *Systems of Family and Marital Psychotherapy*, New York, Brunner/Mazel.

Stern, D. (1977) *The First Relationship: Infant and Mother*, London, Fontana/Open Books.

Tattum, D. P. (1982) *Disruptive Pupils in Schools and Units*, Chichester, Wiley.

Tizard, J., Schofield, W. N. and Hewison, J. (1982) 'Collaboration between teachers and parents in assisting children's reading', *British Journal of Educational Psychology*, 52, part 1.

Tucker, B. Z. and Dyson, E. (1966) 'The family and the school. Utilising human resources to promote learning', *Family Processes*, 15, 125–41.

Wachtel, P. (1977) *Psycho-analysis and Behavior Therapy: Towards a Theory of Integration*, New York, Basic Books.

Walczak, Y. and Burns, S. (1984) *Divorce: The Child's Point of View*, London, Harper & Row.

Walrond-Skinner, S. (1976) *Family Therapy: The Treatment of Natural Systems*, London, Routledge & Kegan Paul.

Watzlawick, P. (1978) *The Language of Change: Elements of Therapeutic Communication*, New York, Basic Books.

Watzlawick, P., Beavin, J. H. and Jackson, D. D. (1968) *Pragmatics of Human Communication. A Study of Interactional Patterns, Pathologies and Paradoxes*, London, Faber & Faber.

Wedge, P. and Prosser, H. (1973) *Born to Fail?*, London, Arrow Books in association with National Children's Bureau.

Willan, S. and Hugman, Y. (1982) 'Family therapy', *Journal of the Association of Educational Psychologists*, 5(8).

Winnicott, D. W. (1965a) *The Family and Individual Development*, London, Tavistock.

Winnicott, D. W. (1965b) 'The parent–infant relationship', in *The Maturational Process and the Facilitating Environment*, London, Hogarth Press.

Name index

Subject index